Teaching the
Language-different Child
to Read

The Charles E. Merrill
COMPREHENSIVE READING PROGRAM

Arthur W. Heilman
Consulting Editor

TEACHING THE LANGUAGE-DIFFERENT CHILD TO READ

CARMEN A. O'BRIEN

Arizona State University

CHARLES E. MERRILL PUBLISHING COMPANY

A Bell & Howell Company   Columbus, Ohio

371.97

$O_b\,6\,t$

Published by
Charles E. Merrill Publishing Company
A Bell & Howell Company
Columbus, Ohio 43216

Library of Congress Catalog Card Number: 72–96027

International Standard Book Number: 0–675–08979–4

2 3 4 5 6 7 8 9 10—77 76

PRINTED IN THE UNITED STATES OF AMERICA

Preface

In spite of the fact that reading problems have probably been given more attention than any area in the elementary education curriculum, there are yet thousands of students in the United States who read so poorly as to be classified as functionally illiterate. It is no secret that the majority of that group are children for whom English is a second language. While schools cannot be held totally accountable for this problem, the burden of finding solutions falls heavily on the shoulders of teachers who work with primary children. One assumption seems clear. Methods and materials designed to teach English-speaking monolinguals to read have not been effective for children with significant language differences.

This book is designed for teachers at the pre-service and in-service level of teaching. The materials of the text have been prepared with some specific purposes in mind:

1. to point up the relationship between language and culture,
2. to alert teachers to the contrasts of sound and structure in different language systems,
3. to show how language difference can interfere with a child's ability to cope with reading in a second language system,
4. to assist teachers in implementing strategies that link reading to listening, speaking and writing, and
5. to suggest ways to humanize and personalize reading instruction.

The first half of the book draws heavily on linguistic and psychological studies to show how language works and how children learn language. The second half offers practical techniques for teaching reading through a communication-experience approach. Special emphasis is placed on beginning steps in the reading program. Suggestions for individualizing instruction through classroom organization and utilization of people resources are offered throughout the book.

I'm deeply grateful to all the teachers who have inspired me with creative ideas for teaching reading. I wish to express particular appreciation to Mrs. Marietta Coffin who contributed the children's writing that appears in the book. During the preparation of the material John O'Brien offered helpful counsel and suggestions based upon his many years of work with Indian students. I'm sincerely grateful.

If in any way the ideas presented in this book help teachers find ways to better cope with their tremendously important role in causing children to become competent readers, my purposes will have been fulfilled.

Carmen O'Brien

TO JOHN, WHO UNDERSTOOD

Contents

The Right
to Literacy

To the person who regards reading as an accepted part of everyday activity, it is difficult to realize that there are at least three million adults in the United States who are totally unable to read or write. Furthermore, according to the United States Office of Education estimates, as reported by Cassels, "there are upwards of 20 million others—young and old— who are such poor readers as to be functionally illiterate,"[1] a shocking 10 percent of the U.S. population.

In editorial comment, Cassels points up the seriousness of this "crippling handicap":

> The illiterate can't fill out the papers necessary to apply for a job, or for unemployment compensation. He can't read the newspapers so he may not know about things—such as food stamps or free health services—that the government makes available to relieve his poverty. He can't vote, or get a driver's license, or read his mail, even if it happens to include something very important, such as a foreclosure notice.[2]

Few desirable positions are open to those with only an elementary education. The high school diploma secures limited opportunity for employment—in fact, many workers are denied employment training because of lack of education. Dropout rates continue to rise in the high

---

[1]Louis Cassels, "Literacy Efforts Short of Funds," United Press International, *Phoenix Gazette,* February 24, 1972, p. 52.

[2]*Ibid.*

1

schools in less privileged areas and the vicious problems of illiteracy, unemployment, discrimination, and job dissatisfaction persist. DeBoer and Dallmann in considering the problem, state that:

> No one claims that elimination of illiteracy will cure all evils of unemployment, discrimination, low standards of living, or problems of child rearing . . . but educational requirements are mounting.[3]

While functional literacy is not regarded as a cure-all by these writers they believe that ". . . low educational attainment is cause for serious concern."[4]

While illiteracy is undeniably related to unemployment, there are other problems of social and political significance that are equally serious. Many citizens are disadvantaged in their civic and social relationship because they are illiterate. In the past decade language has become a powerful weapon. Today's citizen is caught up in intricate webs spun from the fibers of mass media. Man's ability to claim the privileges of individual freedom and social equality depends in large measure on his ability to work through the maze by fully utilizing his power to think critically, to read productively, and to express himself boldly.

THE OBLIGATION OF LITERACY

The premise that every human being should be guaranteed the right of literacy generally receives quick acceptance. Another premise, not so readily accepted, is that language is an obligation reaching beyond the personal domain—a notion that says one's language is not one's own business. Such a premise implies first, that the language producer has an obligation to his listener or reader for accurate, honest, responsible use of the language; second, that any member of a social group is obliged to use his literacy skills to increase his capabilities and exercise his civic responsibilities as a functioning citizen; and finally, that literate people should assume a sense of trusteeship for their language—not only to preserve the unique qualities of language, but to extend, enrich, and enhance them. Beyond the primary goal of guaranteeing the individual's right to literacy, education must view with equal concern the objectives

---

[3]John J. DeBoer and Martha Dallmann, *The Teaching of Reading* (New York: Holt, Rinehart, and Winston, Inc., 1964), p. 532.
[4]*Ibid.*

of developing language appreciation, language pride, and literary sensitivity.

THE DEFINITION OF LITERACY

In the present decade, literacy, by its broad definition, has limited value and is not an end in itself. Literacy is a personal, social, civic issue. Individually and collectively we are charged with the responsibility of extending literacy to the functional level. Perhaps that level is best described by a statement formulated by UNESCO at the 1965 conference in Teheran as strategies were adopted for the World Literacy Program:

> Rather than an end in itself, literacy should be regarded as a way of preparing man for a social, civic, and economic role that goes far beyond the limits of rudimentary literacy training consisting of teaching reading and writing. The very process of learning to read and write should be an opportunity for acquiring information that can immediately be used to improve living standards: reading and writing should lead not only to elementary knowledge, but to training for work, increased productivity, a greater participation in civic life, and a better understanding of the surrounding world, and should ultimately open the way to basic human culture.

THE PROBLEM

Neither platitudes nor explanations alter the fact that at least 10 percent of our citizens aged 14 years or older cannot read or write at a functional level. There are countless reasons for this tragedy, but we need only examine statistics to locate some of the critical factors relating to it.

For example, according to Strom, 270,000 persons in Cook County, Illinois were on public assistance in 1965. "Fifty percent of the Chicago reliefers cannot read and write at eighth grade level" and " . . . over half of that group are under 32 years of age and because of their youth may be expected to produce another generation of dropouts."[5]

The situation is similar in underprivileged areas throughout the country. Illiteracy figures run high among impoverished inner city dwellers. School dropouts are on the increase in ghetto areas. The endless

---

[5]Robert D. Strom, *Teaching in the Slum School* (Columbus, Ohio: Charles E. Merrill Publishing Company, 1965), p. 98.

cycle persists. The problem, as Strom sees it, is "desire without competence";[6] unemployed youth looking for work but unqualified to secure or hold positions even though jobs may exist. Lack of reading ability and poor oral communication ability are a part of that problem.

Kobrick, in an article in *Saturday Review*, cites statistics he believes to be critical. According to his report, the U.S. Office of Education estimates that five million children attending public schools speak a language other than English in their homes and neighborhoods. In New York City, 250,000 Puerto Rican children attend public schools and the estimated dropout rate for these students is said to be as high as 85 percent. "As many as half of Boston's 10,000 Spanish-speaking school children were not in school."[7] (The ages of these children were not given.)

Between two and three million Spanish-speaking children attend school in the five Southwestern states and the average number of school years completed by the Chicanos in the Southwest is 7.1 years. It was this group of Chicanos who, according to Kobrick, successfully campaigned for a bilingual, bicultural education bill which was passed in 1965.

The Bilingual Education Act provides for financial assistance to local education agencies for programs in bilingual education. Massachusetts passed the nation's first comprehensive state bilingual education law. That law declares that all districts must provide bilingual education programs for children whose native language is not English.

IS BILINGUAL EDUCATION THE ANSWER?

Bilingual education provides that both the native tongue and English be used as mediums of education. In such a program, children are taught to read their native language at the same time they are learning to speak, write and read English. The native language is maintained as a functional part of classroom instruction. Kobrick, making an eloquent plea for allowing the child to begin his schooling in the language he knows best, declares that the "English-only" approach ". . . can cause permanent harm by literally jamming the only intellectual channel available to him when he arrives at school."[8]

---

[6]Strom, p. 97.

[7]Jeffrey W. Kobrick, "The Compelling Case for Bilingual Education," *Saturday Review* 55, no. 18 (April 29, 1972): 54.

[8]Kobrick, p. 58.

One of the reasons that bilingual schools have been slow to develop is the diversity of languages among school enrollees in a given school district. It is not unusual for students in a single classroom to represent not two, but three or four different language groups.

In many classrooms in the Southwest, class enrollees may include Indian children, Mexican-American children, Negro children, and inner city ghetto speakers who may be white or black. The question then is not one of bilingualism—it is multilingual-multiculturalism. If the word overpowers you, think what is implied in implementing the program.

WHERE DO WE GO FROM HERE?

You will recall that Alice, in Lewis Carroll's classic, asked of the cat,

"Will you please tell me which way I ought to go from here?"

"That depends a great deal on where you want to get," answered the cat.

"I don't much care where . . ." said Alice.

"Then it doesn't matter which way you go," said the cat.

". . . so long as I get somewhere," Alice added as an explanation.

"Oh, you're sure to do that," said the cat, "if only you walk long enough."

It would appear that we cannot afford to take an Alice in Wonderland position. Prospects for insuring that all mentally capable people may claim full right to functional literacy depends a great deal on the type of education the child receives at the primary level in elementary school. It matters a great deal which way we go from here, for unless the young child can cope with communication skills with a degree of success and self-satisfaction, it is unlikely that he will continue his education beyond compulsory school age.

It is clear that critical problems remain to be solved. Differences in language systems create problems for readers of any foreign language. For all intents and purposes, English is a foreign language to children who have internalized a non-English linguistic system and can barely understand or speak English. But language is only a part of the problem.

For hundreds of children entering school each year, the "inside school" and the "outside school" are worlds apart. When language difference and socio-cultural difference become a handicap to students, it is because the expectations of the school are unrealistic and curricular planning is short-sighted.

Reading is the sensitive area in this entire arena. Because reading is the secondary process of speech, it is totally enmeshed in the culture and the language of the student. We do not read "reading." We read "speech."

The problems appear to focus upon these critical issues:

1. For some students school represents an alien environment.
2. The linguistic system used by the student may come in conflict with the standard English system of the school.
3. The socio-cultural background of the child may furnish frames of reference significantly different from the context of materials used in instruction.
4. Language is an inseparable part of culture—it is as personal as one's name. To deprecate one's language is to deprecate personal worth.
5. It takes time to reach proficiency in a second language.
6. A program that prematurely forces reading on a student before he is reasonably proficient in speaking the language is a high-risk venture.

CHAPTER 1

When Cultural Backgrounds Differ

Within any cultural setting, customs, habits, beliefs, and values often differ dramatically from home to home, and from neighborhood to neighborhood. A ten minute drive from any given point in a community may reveal significant cultural contrasts. Side by side on the seat of a school bus may be one child from a home that provides lavish comforts and wide cultural experiences, and another from a home where hunger and economic deprivation are as predictable as tomorrow's sunrise.

Needless to say, deprivation can exist in either setting. Far too often the term "disadvantaged" is associated with the conditions of poverty. The "advantaged" child may be one from a two-room hut whose parents care deeply about him and offer the kind of love and emotional support that nourishes self-esteem, security, and integrity. Negative self-concepts, insecurity, rejection and feelings of inferiority thrive in any condition where parents or peers are so wrapped up in personal concerns that they deny children the basic needs of belonging and being loved. Common sense tells us that the conditions of this kind of deprivation can exist in homes of the so-called "upper class" as well as in those of the so-called "lower class." Poverty can create critical situations of deprivation, but deprivation is a general term which is not synonymous with poverty.

Economic deprivation in itself is not the critical issue. Many of the world's outstanding leaders and creative thinkers have grown up in economically deprived conditions. Whether a person strives for high goals appears to relate more to the concept he has of himself than to any other single factor. Symonds has said that he who values himself highly will strive for high goals while he who has a low opinion of himself will be content with mediocre attainments.[1]

Basically, we're speaking of an endless chain of personal-social relationships. Change is inevitable and always has been. Differences in geographic, social, and linguistic backgrounds affect all human behavior. Ethnic backgrounds, cultural values, and parental influences shape a child's frame of reference and consequently determine whether he will view a learning situation as a threat, as a matter of importance, or as a challenge.[2] This is the concept educators must deal with and the implications for teaching are limitless.

SUCCESSFUL STUDENTS ARE SELF-LEARNERS

The effects of automation, technical advances, urban living, and the rapid economic changes on both the national and international scene will demand more and more of the individual in terms of his ability to compete in the labor market, cope with social change, and yet maintain vigorous mental and emotional health. His chances for productive living depend to a large degree on his abilities as a self-learner. The student who graduates from elementary school as a dependent learner already has three strikes against him. He is "fair game" for exploitation, his chances for vocational choice are already limited, and his potential for creative, worthy citizenship is in question.

BAND-AIDS ARE NOT ENOUGH

Bloom predicts that rapid social changes will require a new conception of the task of schools, a new orientation to teacher training, new developments in curriculum methods and teaching materials, and new viewpoints about the role of the teacher, the administrator, and even the parents. His findings reveal the tremendous importance of the first few years of life for all that follows. Change, according to Bloom, becomes more and more difficult with increasing age and only the most powerful environmental conditions are likely to produce significant changes at later stages of life.[3]

---

[1]Percival M. Symonds, *The Ego and the Self* (New York: Appleton Century Crofts, 1951), p. 25.

[2]*Ibid.*

[3]B. S. Bloom, *Stability and Change in Human Characteristics* (New York: Wiley and Sons, 1964), p. 48.

In light of this, the emphasis on remedial courses on the current scene serves somewhat as a "band-aid" on an inflamed area. The solutions for dealing with learning failure are not in treating the results of disabilities, but in preventing the failure in the first place, early in the student's school experience. Methods of reading instruction for the disadvantaged learner are undergoing change, but that change has been slow to come, partly because of the wide divergence of children's experiences and partly because of the divergence of teachers' backgrounds. Educators often find themselves disadvantaged because of lack of experience to deal with problems that are rapidly emerging.

Just as the student's frame of reference often prevents him from fully utilizing his school learning experiences, the teacher's frame of reference may limit him in designing suitable learning experiences for the disadvantaged learner. We agree with Bloom, who suggests that there must be "a shift in the conception of education as a status-giving and selective system, to a system that develops each individual to his highest potential".[4] Instructional methods aimed toward the "wide middle" with the hope that the fringe learners will somehow catch on eventually is no longer acceptable.

PRONE TO SCHOOL FAILURE

Predominate in the group of students who fail in school or who become dropouts (either figuratively or functionally) are those whose early experiences in the home failed to motivate them toward school-oriented tasks. In some homes, the realities of the here and now make books and school tasks seem quite irrelevant to daily living. Many students labeled as culturally deprived may simply have experiences in homes and neighborhoods which do not transmit the cultural pattern necessary for the types of learning characteristic of the school. In such homes the adults may have a minimum education and hold low expectations for themselves or their children.

Countless youngsters grow up in homes where the only reading material is the comic book pulled from trash cans in the alley, and communication consists of two word commands of "Hurry up," "Commere," "Get goin'." Some five-year-olds have never been farther than five miles away from their own home.

Meal time, for many, is not sitting around a table talking, sharing, and making plans with the family. Often it is a popsicle at the corner

[4]B. S. Bloom, Allison Davis and Robert Hess, *Compensatory Education for Cultural Deprivation* (New York: Holt, Rinehart and Winston, 1965), p. 2.

market bought with the dime left on the sink as mother went to work, or a dish of leftover beans and a bottle of soda pop.

In the raucous reality of crowded neighborhoods with dozens of children on their own from dawn to dusk, and many times from dusk to dawn, children are not without experiences, certainly not without social contacts, and are not deprived of emotional stimulation; but somehow those experiences, those contacts, and that type of stimulation seem not to develop the type of perceptual functioning that prepares children to be successful in school.

Deutsch has contributed immeasurably to our understanding of the disadvantaged child and the learning process. His studies of the preschool child have served as a basis for much of the planning for Head Start and early education programs. His point of view has been that:

> The lower class child enters school so poorly prepared to produce what the school demands, that initial failures are almost inevitable, and the school experience becomes negatively rather than positively reinforced.[5]

In studying auditory discrimination in terms of verbalization, Deutsch found that children raised in a very noisy environment with little directed speech are deficient in the discrimination and recognition of speech sounds. Therefore, they generally have difficulty with any skill that is primarily dependent on good auditory discrimination. He cites this and a number of other factors as reasons why "lower-class" children are often unprepared for school tasks:

1. Lack of auditory, visual, and tactile stimulation.
2. Lack of materials or objects to develop visual discrimination skills.
3. Lack of time or opportunity for direct communication and feedback with adults.
4. Lack of expectation of reward for performance.
5. Inability to sustain attention, since most tasks are motoric, have a short time span, and are more likely to be related to concrete objects or services for people.

Along with these factors, of course, are the general conditions of physical health, stamina, and energy. When nutrition and child care are

---

[5]M. Deutsch, "The Disadvantaged Child and the Learning Process," in *Education in Depressed Areas*, ed. A. H. Passow (New York: Teacher's College, Columbia University, 1963), pp. 163–180.

substandard, physical readiness for school tasks becomes an overriding factor. The child whose energy is expended by ten o'clock in the morning because of poor nutrition is unlikely to be motivated by any method or curricular innovation.

Where there are patterns of long-standing poverty, language is apt to be more limited, more oriented toward nonverbal means, and likely to be restricted in the number of grammatical forms. Bernstein postulated linguistic differences associated with social-class membership and later confirmed his predictions. He speaks of two linguistic codes: formal or elaborated, and public or restricted. Most "middle class children," he suggests, learn both formal and public codes—the formal being more grammatically complex and allowing for elaboration of meaning and subjective feelings. Children from the less advantaged environment, he believes, are restricted to the public code which is simple grammatically and does not provide for precise statements of ideas or emotions.

Characteristics of the public code, according to Bernstein's findings, are:

1. Short, simple, often inaccurate sentences
2. Repetitive use of conjunctions
3. Little use of subordinate clauses
4. Limited use of adverbs and adjectives.[6]

In the "prone toward school failure group" are students who look for immediate results and tangible rewards rather than learning for the sake of learning or for deferred rewards. Just as success breeds success, failure breeds failure. If the student continues to fail and is a candidate for remedial groups year after year, he becomes alienated to the entire school situation. Dropouts usually appear early. The second grade child who becomes disenchanted after two years of frustration and failure becomes a functional dropout.

Schools cannot change or solve the problems of poverty or deprivation. Neither can conditions of home environment be controlled by educators. Cultural differences, social differences, individual differences will always exist. What schools can and must do, however, is to emphasize the goals that accept the child as a person of worth and dignity, and then care about him as an individual as he bridges the gap between his own culture and the cultural patterns of others. Tucker describes this as cultural pluralism and says in regard to Indian education:

---

[6]B. Bernstein, "Social Class and Linguistic Development: A Theory of Social Learning," in *Education, Economy and Society,* ed. A. H. Halsey, J. Flound, and C. A. Anderson (Glencoe, Ill.: The Free Press, 1961), pp. 288–314.

We must help the child to live in two cultures . . . to respect his own and to become a contributing citizen of the United States. . . . it is only through respect of his own culture that a child is rendered emotionally secure and confident.[7]

THE TEACHER MAY HAVE A BRIDGE TO CROSS

The gap between home and school, pupil and teacher, pupil and pupil is all too often wide and deep. Bridges have to be built strong enough and wide enough to span those gaps. Such a bridge must have a sign at both ends, "Enter Here," for there must be two-way passage. No bridge leads only one way. Education must be the bridge that leads to new experiences and new understanding without cutting off or depreciating values, beliefs, or customs of the outside school environment. Teachers who work in school communities where values and customs differ from their own backgrounds often discover that they are unprepared for problems they face. Too often, it is the teacher who is disadvantaged.

Conventional methods and traditional text materials are rarely suited to the needs of the culturally different child. Often teachers blame themselves when failures result. While it may be true that some teachers are simply better "constituted" to work with the so-called "average" child than with "special need" children, more often than not they simply are untrained for the specialized task and are without the support of materials and aids designed for disadvantaged children.

CONCLUSIONS

Far too often the experiences of one's own environment build a wall that blocks the view beyond. The teacher who has neither seen nor sensed the conditions of deprivation finds it difficult to understand the behavior of a child who comes to school limited by a circle of poverty. Equally perplexing may be the problems involved in meeting the needs of the child whose background is non-English or whose cultural experiences differ significantly from the school environment.

Teachers find themselves in the role of culture and language mediators for students who by necessity must become bi-cultural if they are

---

[7]Abraham Tucker, in the *Gallup Branch of Indian Affairs Bulletin,* New Mexico Area Office, 1965. (Published periodically as a teacher service bulletin.)

to cope with the social and economic problems that are an inevitable part of transition. The acculturation process cannot take place within the four walls of a classroom. The teacher must serve as a bridge between the student's own cultural background and experiences and the differing views and experiences of his peers in the classroom.

In this role the teacher must know the school community well in order to enhance multi-cultural relationships. Only when students understand, appreciate, and respect their own cultural heritage can they become productive in a bi-cultural role. Language is an intricate part of that cultural heritage.

One of the miracles of childhood is that there is a universality in child-to-child communication. If adults can resist the passion to structure and control and every moment of natural play and work activity, children will not only ignore socio-cultural barriers, but will pick up each other's language systems rapidly. Then, speech comes first and writing and reading can follow in that order. The key would seem to be in ensuring that children are integrated in such a way that there is a balance between English speakers and second language speakers.

Hopefully, funds will continue to provide for Teacher Aides who speak the language of the monolingual non-English-speaking students. In such one-to-one relationships a child has the benefit of bilingual instruction as the aide and teacher work together. In so doing, there is hope that the native language of the non-English speaker can be maintained, improved, and enhanced. The irony of ignoring the child's "other than English" language for his first five years in school and then requiring him to take a foreign language in high school or college is incomprehensible.

EXTENDED READINGS

Ausubel, D. P. "How Reversible are the Cognitive and Motivational Effects of Cultural Deprivation?" Paper read at Conference on Teaching the Bilingual Child, Buffalo, New York, March, 1963.

Bloom, B. S., A. Davis, and Robert Hess. *Compensatory Education for Cultural Deprivation.* New York: Holt, Rinehart, and Winston, 1965, pp. 12–16, 67–75.

Bossard, James H. S. *Parent and Child: Studies in Family Behavior.* Philadelphia: University of Pennsylvania Press, 1953, Chap. V.

Carroll, J. B. "Language Development," in *Encyclopedia of Educational Research,* edited by C. W. Harris. New York: Macmillan, 1960.

DeBoer, John J., and Martha Dallmann. *The Teaching of Reading.* New York: Holt, Rinehart and Winston, 1970, pp. 24–25.

Deutsch, M., and B. Brown. "Social Influences in Negro-White Intelligence Differences." *Journal of Social Issues* 20, no. 2 (1964):24–35.

Ells, K. *Intelligence and Cultural Differences.* Chicago: University of Chicago Press, 1951.

Flavel, J. H. *The Developmental Psychology of Jean Piaget.* Princeton: Van Nostrand, 1963.

Gill, L. J., and B. Spilka. "Some Non-intellectual Correlates of Academic Achievements Among Mexican-American Secondary School Students." *Journal of Educational Psychology* 53(1962):144–149.

Hebb, D. O. "Heredity and Environment in Mammalian Behavior." *British Journal of Animal Behavior* 1(1953):43–47.

————. *The Organization of Behavior.* New York: John Wiley and Sons, 1949.

Inhelder, Barbel, and Jean Piaget. *The Growth of Logical Thinking From Childhood to Adolescence.* Translated by A. Parsons and S. Milgram. New York: Basic Books, 1958.

Kobrick, Jeffrey W. "The Compelling Case for Bilingual Education." *Saturday Review* 40, no. 2 (April 29, 1972):54–58.

Lewis, Hylan. "Child Rearing Among Low Income Families in the District of Columbia." Presented at the National Conference on Social Welfare, Minneapolis, Minnesota, May 16, 1961. Mimeographed.

Maslow, A. H. "A Theory of Human Motivation." *Psychological Review* 50(1943):370–396.

McCarthy, Dorothea. *Language Development of the Pre-school Child,* Inst. Child Welfare Monograph No. 4 (Minneapolis, 1930).

Plant, James S. "Family Living Space and Personality Development." in *A Modern Introduction to the Family,* ed. Norman W. Bell and Ezra F. Vogel. Glencoe, Ill.: The Free Press, 1960.

Strom, Robert D. *Teaching in the Slum School.* Columbus, Ohio: Charles E. Merrill Publishing Company, 1965, Chapters 1, 2, and 5.

————. "What is the School Speed-up Doing to Children?" *The Elementary School Journal* 65, no. 4 (January 1965):206–7.

————. "Are These Our Ugly Americans?" *Kentucky School Journal* 43, no. 2 (October 1964):20–22, 46.

CHAPTER 2

What the Linguist Says to the Reading Teacher

I stopped at my favorite roadside stand in the Japanese gardens that fringe the outskirts of my town. While waiting to have a bouquet of flowers arranged, I watched a petite, dark-haired girl who appeared to be around four years of age dart between tables of carnations and baskets of fresh ripe tomatoes.

Tiny feet paused at the sorting tables. "Aye! Tengo mucho hambre. Mi gustan mucho las strawberries. Da me un poco de strawberries para comer." Pirouetting first on one toe and then the other, she continued in rapid-fire Spanish to persuade the busy worker. Rewarded with one glossy, plump strawberry, she continued her explorations, pausing to exchange affection with a small kitten.

From the back door of the shop, an older man spoke to her in a tongue totally unfamiliar to me. Quickly the child skipped to the check-out counter. "Mom, Grandfather wants me to go to market with him in the truck. Can I go please?" Her English was clear and precise.

A quick nod from her mother and a last minute, "Kumika, wash your face first," brought a pleading look and an appeal, "Mom, Grandfather said, 'Hurry!' " A non-relenting look sent Kumika toward a dripping faucet.

As I reached for my sales slip, I questioned Kumika's dark-haired mother. "Does your little girl speak both English and Spanish?" "Oh! yes, and Japanese too. You see, she is with her grandfather and grandmother much of the day. They speak only Japanese. But my husband and I speak only English to her."

15

Deftly punching the cash register with one hand and giving the floral arrangement a last adjustment with the other, she continued. "Most of Kumika's little friends speak Spanish. She usually plays with Mrs. Morales' children here at the market."

I was unable to curb my curiosity. "Which language does she prefer? Which is the one she uses automatically?" I asked. Her answer surprised me.

"I don't know. I haven't thought about that! She uses whichever language she needs whenever she wishes."

In the primary classroom Kumika is soon to enter, she is likely to be the only student who will be functional in three linguistic systems. Among her classmates will be students who can understand English to a limited degree, but are functional in Spanish only. Many will be using both nonstandard English and nonstandard Spanish. Still others will be using a dialect that makes standard English, for all intents and purposes, a second language.

Those who teach in communities where linguistic backgrounds differ significantly from standard English and socio-ethnic backgrounds differ significantly from that of the typical middle-class Anglo-American, must be prepared to answer such questions as follows:

1. What is the nature of language?
2. How is language acquired?
3. What happens as a second language learner shifts from one linguistic system to another?
4. How do bilinguals compare to monolinguals in linguistic attainment?
5. What is defective speech?
6. Is there a direct relationship between speech defects and reading proficiency?
7. Is dialectical difference a barrier in the reading process?

LINGUISTICS IS A SCIENCE

The term "linguistics" has been bandied about in the past few years as if it were a method of teaching, and sometimes as if it were a newly discovered branch of study. Moulton describes linguistics as the study of language as it changes through time, varies through space, and differs from one social group to another.[1] "A linguist . . . is a student of human languages, a scholar-scientist, whose work is . . . understanding and de-

---

[1] William G. Moulton, "Linguistics and Language Teaching in the United States 1940–1960" (Washington, D.C.: U.S. Government Printing Office, 1962).

scribing the nature of human languages, including its functioning processes," says Pose Lamb.[2]

The diversity of theories held by linguists is obvious. The breadth and scope of language study makes this inevitable. Much confusion exists as teachers attempt to interpret and implement linguistic information. Out of all the deliberations, however, have come some understandings about language that have set some new directions in reading methods. Particularly for teachers who work with second language learners, some of the basic descriptions of the nature of language helps to put reading in proper perspective.

We need the support of scientific research to help us devise realistic methods of instruction in this specialized field. While there is great need for continued research in the area, a wealth of information is available to us from related fields. We need to look to the psychologist for help in understanding how the child develops, to seek out the psycho-linguist for insights of language and the intellectual processes, and we need the linguist's description of the phonological and structural aspects of language.

Many new programs designed for second language learning are being published. Teachers cannot afford to accept them on blind faith. Some are exciting and productive, but far too many were hurriedly put on the market and already have been reconsidered, revised and some rejected. Many failed to achieve any significant change from traditional reading and language programs, perhaps because psycho-social factors were not taken into account. Programs must fit the child—it is not the other way around.

Programs have, on the other hand, failed many times because teachers have not had enough help in understanding the problems of second language learning. Often because of the external pressure, teachers have pushed pupils into reading, which is the secondary form of language, before they have developed functional competence in speech, which is the primary form of language. In a sense, the pressure may be more internal than external, for teachers often seem to have trouble in resisting the passion to get a reading book into the hands of a pupil, even though his English speaking competence may be limited to, "Guh morning," "Guh 'bye," and "Me wants ta play wi' da truck."

Language is Personal

Linguists have made us acutely aware that language is probably the most complex of all intellectual processes, yet by some strange miracle,

---

[2]Lamb, Pose, *Linguistics in Proper Perspective* (Columbus, Ohio: Charles E. Merrill Pub. Co., 1967), p. 3.

most children manage to have mastered the basic system of the sound and structure of speech by the age of four or five. There seems to be little doubt that the infant comes into the world innately equipped to talk, physically, neurologically, and mentally, and unless some unnatural cause intervenes, he will continue to do so until the day he dies.

The language patterns the child learns in those early years are enmeshed in the totality of his psycho-social behavior. They become an inseparable part of his personality, whether the language is French, Spanish, Dutch, Navajo, English, or any other. That language, the native tongue, is learned in a period of rapid intellectual development when according to some studies, the mind is highly receptive to speech pattern development. That language is personal! It becomes habitual! It will not be easily changed!

Language has an Evolutionary Nature

Language usage differs from group to group. Dialectical patterns develop within speech communities that become acceptable as standard speech. The change is a natural consequence of social change.

Changes which occur in linguistic patterns within speech communities are not haphazard or accidental. They can be mapped and charted. Furthermore, as Lamb puts it, "The changes which occur are not indicative of decay or degeneration, but rather they are hallmarks of a living, growing, healthy organism."[3]

Speech is the Primary Form of Language

The child learns to "talk" his native language somewhere between the ages of two and five by using patterns of vocal noises to communicate his needs, to share his feelings, and to satisfy his pleasures. Writing is the graphic representation of language. Reading is the process of decoding those graphic symbols to the sounds of speech.

Language is Systematic

All languages have two systems that make up the code of that language—one is a system of sounds and one is a system of meanings.[4] We can understand and produce that language when we can use the signals within each system.

---

[3]Lamb, p. 17.

[4]Ronald Wardhaugh, "Study of Language," in *Language and Learning to Read,* ed. Richard E. Hodges and E. Hugh Rudorf (Boston: Houghton Mifflin Company, 1972), p. 14.

Language Signals

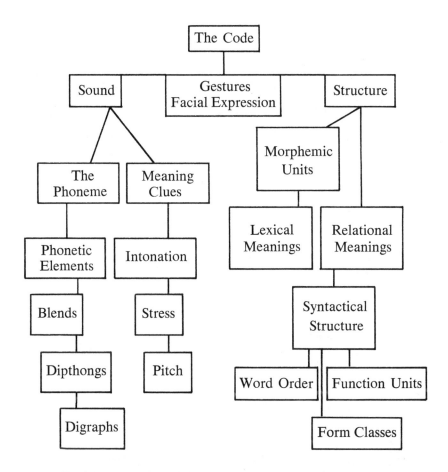

Each language has distinctive systems of sound, grammar, and vocabulary that have been arbitrarily determined:

- *phonemic patterns,* the smallest units of sound in an utterance (cat *kat*) (church *ch r ch*)
- *morphemic patterns,* the meaning-bearing units within a word (boys *boy s*) (unlocking *un lock ing*)
- *syntactical patterns,* phrases and sentences.

The clue to language meaning is often indicated by:
- *stress,* the speaker's voice volume
- *pitch,* highness or lowness of voice sound

— *juncture,* the pauses or partial pauses connecting parts of utterances

— *non-verbal communication* in the form of gestures, movement, or facial expression.

Language is Arbitrary

To become functional in a language, we must be able to use the signals of both sound and structure to produce or to interpret language. While speech is first learned in streams of sound, each utterance is made up of combinations of phonemes (the smallest unit of sound in any utterance). The symbols of those units of sound (b, bl, bla, spoi, and so on), signal no meaning. Only when they fall into arbitrarily determined structure patterns do we attach meaning.

Although the following letters are arranged in word-like units in the pattern of a sentence, they signal no meaning to you:

htsi a ecnetnes tshro si.

When the letters are reordered and the words rearranged according to the system of sounds and structure of English, you recognize the sentence as,

This is a short sentence.

The clue to language meaning is found in the phonemic, morphemic, and grammatical patterns that have been arbitrarily determined. Although there is flexibility within the system, there are limits within which the process can work or as Wardhaugh puts it, ". . . such units as letters and words, and such processes as sentences, are thought to be constructed according to some 'sense making' formula."[5]

The problem of course for second language learners is that sound and meaning systems differ between languages. The "formula" which works in one language cannot be superimposed on another.

WHEN ENGLISH IS THE SECOND LANGUAGE

Young has pointed up the complexity of second language learning in the following:

Language is not a simple matter of what word is used by one speech system as against another, and language learning is not a

---

[5]Wardhaugh, p. 16.

simple mechanical process of memorizing new vocabulary. The closest approximation to a mechanical process occurs only between very closely related cultural-linguistic communities; but as the range of difference widens, the usefulness of a mechanical approach diminishes. The learner of a new language is, at the same time, inducting himself—or being inducted—into a new world where he must view his relationship with other men, and with the whole environment that surrounds him, in a new and different manner. This is not easy, because the manner to which he has previously accustomed himself has taken on the form of a set of rather rigid habits—and as we all know from experience, habits are not easily modified.

If he was reared in a western European society, speaking an Indo-European language, his world view incorporated a great number of elements and concepts that do not characterize that of a Navajo reared in the canyon country in the back reaches of the reservation, or of an Eskimo at Point Barrow. He is not only accustomed to looking upon a different physical world from that of the Eskimo or the Navajo, but he has formed a different set of habits and concepts regarding the interrelationship of the features of that world and of himself as a part of it.[6]

Meanings are the product of the individual's total experience, some unique to him, others a result of reinforcement he has had from other individuals in his speech community.[7] Moreover, there is a strong element of emotion in verbal behavior.[8] Consequently, the second language learner is often thrust into a complex situation where he must deal with different sets of habits, a new relationship with peers, and a differing frame of reference. Frustration, fear of making a mistake, and feelings of personal inadequacy are likely to result.

LANGUAGE SHIFT

After becoming functionally efficient in his first language, a person who attempts to learn another must deal with new sets of decoding and encoding habits that come into competition with the old. As he shifts

[6]Robert Young, from an address to teachers of the Navajo Agency, Gallup, New Mexico, in October, 1966.

[7]W. Rivers, *The Psychologist and the Foreign Language Teacher* (Chicago: University of Chicago Press, 1964), pp. 27–28.

[8]O. Hobart Mowrer, *Learning Theory and Behavior* (New York: John Wiley and Sons, 1960), p. 71.

from one language to another, the two systems come into conflict with each other.[9] He expects the target language to follow the formula of his first language.

The native "hearer" makes use of predictable or partially predictable items and sequence and so can piece together bits and pieces of utterances to arrive at comprehensible meanings. The second language learner is bereft of clues either from familiar structures such as the order of words in a sentence or the rhythm patterns of words or phrases. He has to hear everything, retain what he hears, and simultaneously grasp meanings. "If he is mentally capable," says Rivers, "highly motivated, and is able to retain what he hears long enough to rehearse it again subvocally and so build up memory traces, he will take all this in his stride.[10] If, however, he is handicapped by any psycho-social factor or pressed beyond his capacity, the interference or negative transfer from the native language is likely to become a serious obstacle.

The interference factor has implications for reading instruction. Is it possible that the language shift is a significant factor in coding skills? If so, the typical phonic instruction program must be carefully examined.

TYPES OF BILINGUALISM

Two types of bilingualism are described by linguists. The types are defined as (1) compound bilinguals and (2) coordinate bilinguals. The compound bilingual has two functionally dependent systems and must use a common thinking process for both languages. The coordinate bilingual has two functionally independent language systems and apparently has relatively distinct thinking processes and symbols in each language. Bilinguals do not reach the coordinate stage without a great deal of practice. Typically this is the individual who relies very little on translation and immerses himself in the living culture of another speech community.[11]

Very few children are coordinate bilinguals. More typically children use one language functionally and can understand and use the second on a limited basis. In most instances, the child uses a common thinking process for both his languages. Presumably he has a dominate functional

---

[9]C. E. Osgood and F. Sebolk (eds.), *Psycholinguistics* (Bloomington, Indiana: University Press, 1965), p. 139.

[10]Rivers, p. 28.

[11]Osgood and Sebolk, pp. 139–146.

language system and his second language is dependent upon the first for translation. Such a person is likely to be constantly cross referencing between languages.

Erwin and Osgood make some predictions that should be very interesting to second language teachers. They predict that if a coordinate bilingual is "hired" to interpret in one direction only from one language to another, he will gradually develop an appropriate set of meanings for signs in the second language and lose his ability to speak the first language. If the coordinate bilingual translates in both directions, he must gradually build up both languages.[12]

It is upon this premise that the bilingual schools are based. Zintz describes bilingual schools as those where two languages are put to work in the conduct of the school. He proposes that the schools "take advantage of the language the child already knows, as well as to make him efficient in the language of the school," so that he will be truly bilingual. He states:

> With the needs around the world so great as they are today for people to communicate across the language barrier, it seems extremely foolish that in the United States the child who brought a language other than English to school has been asked to forget it.[13]

The irony of ignoring the child's native language to the point that he no longer speaks it at functional level is obvious. Most elementary schools support the idea of teaching Spanish, French or some foreign language at the elementary school level, yet nothing has been done to utilize the non-English language of the beginning student.

The older notion once held and perpetuated by schools that bilingual children should not be permitted to use non-English in school has for the most part been dispelled. The problem now appears to be in relation to the parents' understanding of the newer attitude. Too often, parents have the feeling expressed by one Spanish-speaking father who put it this way: "I speak only English to my boy now that he is in school. My wife does not speak English very well so she feels very bad. We tell him he must talk in English now." How tragic that such opportunities for school-home cooperation are not utilized as a means of helping the child become a truly functional bilingual!

---

[12]Leon A. Jacobovitz and Wallace E. Lambert, "Semantic Satiation Among Bilinguals," *Journal of Experimental Psychology* 62(1961):576–582.

[13]Miles Zintz, *The Reading Process, The Teacher and the Learner* (Dubuque, Iowa: William C. Brown Co., 1970), p. 325.

WHEN SPEECH IS DEFECTIVE

According to Kirk:

> Only speech which deviates from the average so far as to draw unfavorable attention to the speaker, whether through unpleasant sound, inappropriateness to the age level, or lack of intelligibility, may be classified as defective.[14]

While there is much controversy concerning "correctness or incorrectness" of speech, particularly as related to ghetto speech or regional dialect, the fact remains that the child cannot be taught to read standard English unless he hears and speaks a reasonable approximation of English sounds. We might say then that any speech which deviates from standard English pronunciation to the degree that it interferes with the coding of English symbols to English sounds may be classified as defective insofar as reading standard English is concerned. Until and unless the child can approximate the sounds of English in his speech, he cannot profit from phonic instruction.

"Correcting" speech deviations in English need not be replacement of a child's speech patterns. To tell a child his way is wrong is to deprecate not only his language system but his self-image. Teaching English as an alternate means that the teacher simply says, "Here is another way to say it." After all, the truly educated individual is the person who can function linguistically in whatever situation he finds himself, without drawing unfavorable attention to his way of speaking.

TYPES OF SPEECH DEVIATION

Deviations may result either from organic factors such as malformation of speech organs, hearing loss, or cerebral dysfunction, or from functional factors associated with environment or emotions.[15]

While research has not clearly indicated whether speech defects affect reading ability, the findings related to functional speech deviation is somewhat more clearly established. Artley[16] concluded that while

---

[14]Samuel A. Kirk, *Educating Exceptional Children* (Boston: Houghton Mifflin Company, 1962), p. 294.

[15]Kirk, p. 294.

[16]A. S. Artley, "A Study of Certain Factors Presumed to be Associated with Reading and Speech Difficulties," *Journal of Speech and Hearing Disorders* 13(December, 1948):359.

there appears to be a relationship between speech difficulties and reading deficiencies, the extent of this relationship is not clear. Monroe[17], on the other hand, found more children with speech defects among poor readers tested than among average readers. However, no conclusive data is available to determine which is the cause and which is the effect.

On the other hand, there is considerable research to indicate causal relationships between bilingualism and reading. Macnamara's review of seventy-five studies revealed that bilinguals have a weaker grasp on oral-aural command of English than monolinguals. Carrow's studies also revealed significant deficiencies among Spanish-English bilinguals in oral reading, comprehension and hearing vocabulary. A higher percentage of articulatory defects was found among the bilingual group as well. Findings such as these indicate that we are justified in our belief that children whose speech deviates significantly from the standard patterns and sounds of English must be introduced to reading through the oral-aural approach.

CONCLUSIONS

Speech is the primary form of language. Writing is the abstract form of speech. Reading is interpreting the meanings intended by the writer.

As the second language learner shifts from one language to another, the two linguistic systems come into conflict. The speaker expects the second language to work in the same way as the native language.

While current testing materials are no doubt slanted in favor of the monolingual, the research evidence from countless studies reveals that the bilingual is inferior in linguistic attainment in his second language to the monolingual. While all the reasons are not clear, those commonly cited are related to:

1. The contrastive features between languages.
2. The difficulty in learning two languages simultaneously.
3. The time factor in second language learning.
4. Home environment and poor speech models.
5. Bicultural factors and differences in experiential background.
6. Attitudes, prejudices, and motivational drive.
7. School practices which fail to provide realistic programs for second language learners.

---

[17]Marion Monroe, *Children Who Cannot Read* (Chicago: University of Chicago Press, 1932).

The relationship between bilingualism and intelligence is a relative matter. The student learning a second language does not have visual, auditory and experiential supports. He has to hear everything and retain it if he is to be successful in his second language. If he is intellectually capable and highly motivated, he will overcome these limitations. If he is uncertain, anxious, has poor auditory discrimination, poor retention, and lacks self-drive, he is severely handicapped in acquiring second-language skill.

Students often approach second language learning with inhibitory attitudes and prejudiced concepts which interfere with achievement. This can be the result of home or social class attitudes. Ironically, many students who are immersed in English in school become embarrassed or reluctant to use the first language and thereby become functionally illiterate in the first language and yet not totally proficient in the second.

Standardized tests developed in English to test students who are monolingual English speakers are not valid instruments for testing students who speak English as their second language.

IMPLICATIONS

Dealing with letter forms, the symbols of language sound, may represent too much too soon for some children. A child cannot read what he cannot perceive auditorily.

Second language learners must be given time for the mediation process while working through the second language. If the learner is pressured for responses before he has time to translate symbols from one system to the other, he is certain to be confused or defeated. He needs the support of analogies, pictures, and realia to furnish clues and reinforcement for new vocabulary meanings.

Teachers need to analyze the contrasts between dominant languages in order to understand the difficulties encountered by second language learners.

More time must be devoted to oral speaking practice if second language learners are to overcome articulatory deviations. Such deviations will not be overcome merely through listening. The teacher is the classroom speech model, but since teachers must divide their time among many students, tape recorders and other recording devices must be utilized to extend time for listening-learning experiences.

Teaching the second language learner must be a highly individualized process. Only in a one-to-one relationship can this pupil reveal his true potential. Only in periods of teacher-pupil interaction can the teacher fulfill the role of guide and counselor.

While evaluation is crucially important for the second language learner, one rarely gets a true measure of this student's ability to achieve or his ability to reason if the testing device used is based on linguistic ability. Too often, the bilingual is handicapped in revealing his potential or demonstrating his competence because he is less able to communicate at the same level of expertness as his monolingual classmates. If he is sensitive, unsure, or uncomfortable, he is likely to react in one of the following ways:

1. By posing indifference or inattention.
2. By distracting the teacher and peers to avoid classroom performance.
3. By retreating and mentally withdrawing from the situation by saying, "I don't know," or "I don't understand."

EXTENDED READINGS

Baratz, Joan. "Teaching Reading in an Urban Negro School System." in *Teaching Black Children to Read,* ed. Joan Baratz and Roger Shuy. Washington, D.C.: Center for Applied Linguistics, 1969.

Fasold, Ralph, and Walt Wolfram. "Some Linguistic Features of Negro Dialect." in *Teaching Standard English in the Inner City,* ed. Ralph Fasold and Roger Shuy. Washington, D.C.: Center for Applied Linguistics, 1970.

Glazar, Nathan. "The Process and Problems of Language Maintenance." in *Language Loyalty in the United States,* ed. J. A. Fishman. New York: Mouton and Company, 1966.

Goodman, Kenneth. "Dialect Barriers to Reading Comprehension." *Elementary English* 42, no. 8 (1965):853–860.

Gumperz, J. J. "Linguistic and Social Interaction in Two Communities." *American Anthropologist* 66, no. 2 (1964):137–153.

Hodges, Richard E., and E. Hugh Rudorf, eds. *Language and Learning to Read.* Boston: Houghton Mifflin Company, 1972.

Jacobovitz, Leon A., and Wallace E. Lambert. "Semantic Satiation Among Bilinguals." *Journal of Experimental Psychology* 62(1961):576–582.

Jones, W. R. "A Critical Study of Bilingualism and Non-verbal Intelligence." *British Journal of Educational Psychology* 30:71–77.

Macnamara, John. *Bilingualism and Primary Education.* Edinburg: University Press, 1966.

Peal, E., and W. E. Lambert. "The Relation of Bilingualism to Intelligence." *Psychological Monographs, General and Applied* 546(1962):72.

Shuy, Roger W. "A Linguistic Background for Developing Beginning Reading Materials for Black Children." in *Teaching Black Children to Read,* ed. Joan Baratz and Roger Shuy. Washington, D.C.: Center for Applied Linguistics, 1969.

Shuy, R. W., J. C. Baratz, and W. A. Wolfram. *Sociolinguistic Factors in Speech Identification.* National Institute of Mental Health Research Project No. MH–15048–01. Washington, D.C.: Center for Applied Linguistics, 1969.

Stewart, William. "On the Use of Negro Dialect in the Teaching of Reading." in *Teaching Black Children to Read,* ed. Joan Baratz and Roger Shuy. Washington, D.C.: Center for Applied Linguistics, 1969.

Venezky, Richard. "Nonstandard Language and Reading." *Elementary English* 47(1970):334–45.

Wolfram, Walt. "Reading Alternatives for Nonstandard Speakers: A Sociolinguistic Perspective." Washington, D.C.: Center for Applied Linguistics, 1970. Mimeographed.

Wolfram, Walt. "Sociolinguistic Implications for Educational Sequencing." in *Teaching Standard English in the Inner City,* ed. Ralph Fasold and Roger Shuy. Washington, D.C.: Center for Applied Linguistics, 1970.

CHAPTER 3

The
Sounds
of English

Book Talk	*Child Talk*
This is Linda.	Thas' Linda.
Linda has a puppy named Ruff.	Linda gotsa puppy.
The puppy is brown with white spots.	He beez wite wif brown 'pots.
Linda is giving the puppy a bath.	Linda begivindapuppy a baf.
Bob is helping Linda.	Bob behelpin Linda.
Ruff is not happy.	Ruff he ain't happy.

To an inner city child using a ghetto dialect, the printed story on the left sounds incorrect and the story on the right represents a social dialect which is comfortable and correct to the speaker. Both are the sounds of language. Both communicate. Both are recognized by linguistic communities as conventional speech. The questions are:

1. What happens to the reading process when the sound patterns of the child's linguistic system do not correspond to the sound systems of standard English?
2. How can we analyze the contrasts between English and other linguistic systems?
3. When does "dialect" become a barrier to school success?

Language is a continuum of speech sound. As described by Trauger:

> It is, as viewed in structural linguistics, a stream or continuum of organized sound that is punctuated (one could say orchestrated) by breaks or junctures of various lengths, stresses, pitches, and gestures.[1]

Certainly not all the sounds of language have to do with organized speech. Owens, discussing the sound system of language, says that it is obvious that some sounds of speech contribute nothing to meaning and that "we could do without the 'ahs' and 'ohs' many of our friends insert in their speech," as well as "the clicking of dentures."[2] Perhaps it can only be said that such extraneous sounds contribute in a sense to meaning by revealing the feelings and attitudes of the speaker *or* the listener.

The sound system of a language includes all those elements that transmit meaning. Such meaning-carrying units are organized as sound patterns. Vowels and consonants are merely arbitrarily chosen characters that are symbols for speech sounds.

The mechanics of the English language are complex in many respects. Not only is there inconsistency in letter-sound correspondence, but there are significant regional dialect differences that alter sound patterns within the United States. The soft drawl of the Southerner's "Ya all come on down, ya heah!" is in sharp contrast to the Easterner's clipped, "Mutha and Ahnt Estah oppose that ideer with vigah!"

Furthermore, if the idea is accepted that communication has to do with the transmission of feelings and emotions, then the sound system must include all the facets of stress or accent, pitch, junctures, and melodic voice rhythm.

Voice stress and tone, for example, may hold the key to meaning. With emphasis on the underlined words, the meaning of each of the following sentences shifts:

1. *This* is the hat I ordered.
2. This *is* the hat I ordered!

---

[1]Wilmer K. Trauger, *Language Arts in the Elementary School* (New York: McGraw-Hill Book Company, 1963), p. 149.

[2]George Owen, "Linguistics: An Overview," in *Readings in Language Arts,* ed. Verna D. Anderson, Paul Anderson, and others (New York: The Macmillan Company, 1964), p. 24.

3. This is the *hat* I ordered?
4. This is the hat *I* ordered!

Eye expression too, is a facet of communication. Try to describe a scene or to be persuasive about a viewpoint while you are blindfolded. Speech, when viewed as a system of sounds and signals, involves all those physical and emotional manifestations that are employed in communicating *meanings, feelings* and *intentions*.

PART I

LETTER-SOUND RELATIONSHIPS

Few of us need to be reminded that there is low correspondence between the symbols and the sounds of the English language. Any nine-year-old struggling with spelling has discovered that the twenty-six letters of the alphabet represent not only the forty-four sounds listed in the pronunciation key of most dictionaries, but countless others occurring in blends, digraphs, dipthongs and phonograms. It is not easy to explain to such a student the reasons why "bed" and "said," "sense" and "cents" or "mean and seen" are spelled differently even though they sound alike, nor why "cough", "tough," "though," and "bough" are spelled similarly even though they are pronounced differently.

A good example of the irregular correspondence of letter-sound relationships is found in the following words: *cat, city, chair, character, chef.* To complicate this irregularity even more, we need only examine the words *service* and *cerus, censor* and *centric* or *succeed* and *secrecy.* Consider too the complications that arise in vowel-consonant letter-sound correspondence. For example, the consonant-vowel pattern "SU" represents six different sounds in the following words.

1. SU/SU, as in *supper*
2. SU/SOO, as in *super*
3. SU/Sə, as in *suppose*
4. SU/SUR, as in *surgery*
5. SU/SWa, as in *suede*
6. SU/shoo, as in *sure*

For a second language learner whose native tongue may not include sounds that correspond to the above, pronunciation and spelling problems may exist.

WHEN SPEECH AND SYMBOLS DON'T MATCH

Elaborate phonic systems have been devised to introduce as logically as possible rules and principles to aid the student in a step-by-step process of decoding symbols to sounds or encoding sounds to symbols. Most phonic systems, however, are based upon the premise that the student speaks English fluently. His task is simply to match his linguistic speech system with the symbols of that system. For many beginning readers, however, such a task is impossible since the code does not have a counterpart in the native tongue.

It is not uncommon to discover students in reading clinics who have been exposed to phonic instruction year after year, yet are not able to attack new words independently. Consider the child who says "shair" for *chair,* yet reverses the process and says "chose" for *shoes.* Before he can code either word, he must deal with the interference factor in his own linguistic system. In the first place, he has a homonym problem; *share* and *chair, chose, choose* and *shoes.* All these words may sound almost the same. In the second place, the digraphs *sh* and *ch* must be interchanged in order to assign sound to symbol. In the third place, he must learn a contradication in order to code the word. He hears *sh* but sees *ch* in *chair,* and he hears *ch* but sees *sh* in *shoes.* Thus, he must cope with a three step process if he is to recognize and pronounce the word *shoes.* Until he "internalizes" the new sounds, coding is impossible.

HELPING SECOND LANGUAGE LEARNERS HEAR THE SOUNDS OF ENGLISH

Reading teachers need to have knowledge of the sound patterns of the language and the mechanical aspects of human production of these sounds. In the teaching of phonics, it is essential to be aware of the motor and kinesthetic factors of speech production. When there is any deviation in speech sound, either because of an organic disorder or a functional disorder retraining is necessary. This is a process that involves kinesthetic training as well as auditory training. A child who has pronounced the word *children* as *shildren* since infancy must become aware of changed placement of tongue and teeth before he can achieve the new sound. In order to help "language-different" learners internalize and make habitual the phonemic system as well as the intonation, stress and rhythm patterns of English, the teacher must:

1. be aware of the production of speech sounds.
2. understand the basic sound system of English.
3. develop competence in analyzing the contrasts between the sound patterns of English and those used by the second language learner.

PART II

INTERFERENCE PROBLEMS—WHEN SPANISH IS THE FIRST LANGUAGE

Some very significant phonemic and grammatical structure differences exist between Spanish and English that pose potential reading problems for the Spanish-language oriented student. In a study guide, *Solutions in Communications,* published by the Santa Clara County Office of Education, a series of practical lessons are built around the following ideas:

1. Children cannot read symbols of sounds they cannot hear.
2. The sound system of Spanish interferes with the acquisition of English in precise ways.
3. These interferences cause problems of clear communication.
4. The task for teachers of Spanish-language oriented children is to know what the points of interference are, then to install the sounds of English as needed.
5. The keenest attention is to be given the problem of word endings.
6. Teachers must learn to hear what the children are truly saying. In other words, they should avoid supplying final sounds that the children are *not* actually saying. Without the mastery of this most vital point, any progress in teaching these students would be seriously hampered.
7. The volume of air flow in all speech must be increased.
8. Some English sounds, which are non-existent in Spanish, must be skillfully installed.
9. Teachers must bear in mind that they are working to *install* the sounds of English, not *replace* Spanish.
10. All educators must be keenly aware that there is a broad spread of abilities in a Spanish-language oriented child with respect to his ability to:

understand, speak, read, and *write* Spanish—
in that precise order.

11. It must be clearly understood that not all Spanish-language
oriented children have problems with all the points of interference.[3]

CONTRASTS BETWEEN THE SPANISH AND
ENGLISH SOUND SYSTEMS

Vowel Sounds

In English	*In Spanish*
The five vowel letters *a, e, i, o,* and *u* represent at least fifteen distinctive phonemes plus blended vowel sounds in the dipthongs, *oi-oy, aw-au, ow-ou, ai-ay.*	Five vowel letters are used to represent five relatively constant sounds:
	a (alto) as heard in *father*
	e (leguna) as heard in *met*
	i(e) (aqui) as heard in *even*
	o (hermosa) as heard in *open*
	u (mucho) as heard in *moon*
English is laced with countless neutral or slurred vowel sounds: (1) *uh,* as in *up* or *cup,* (2) the *schwa* (ə) as heard in *above, melon,* and *brother.*	Spanish has no *uh* sound, nor is the *schwa* heard in the unaccented syllables of words.

It can be predicted that problems will occur with the English vowel
sounds which are nonexistent in Spanish. By using a pronunciation chart
(as shown), it is possible to quickly compare the vowel systems of English and Spanish. As indicated on the "V" below, only five vowel sounds
are heard in Spanish. There is no spoken sound equivalent for the English sounds of ĭ (*it*), ā (*age*), ă (*at*), à (*ask*), *oo* (*foot*), *yoo* (*use*).

Among Spanish-language oriented children who learned English

---

[3]Leonard Olguin, *Solutions in Communications, a T.V. Study Guide* (California: University of Santa Clara, Office of Education, 1972), p. 26.

as a second language or who learned English from second generation parents, the following substitutions occur frequently.

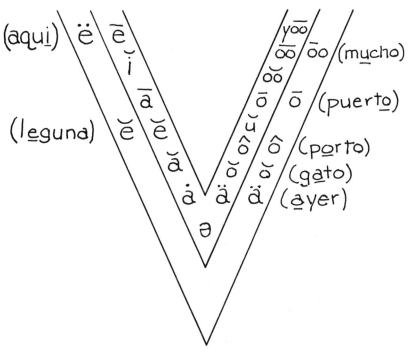

Vowel Sound Substitutions

Short vowel sounds are often interchanged with long vowel sounds:

1. short *i* and long *e* may be interchanged. Short *i* often sounds like *e* (*it>eet*) or (*this>thees*). Long *e* often sounds like *i* (*meal>mill*) or (*feet>fit*).
2. Short *u* often sounds like short *o* (*shut>shot*), (*drum>drahm*), (*brother>brahther*).
3. Short *oo* often sounds like long *oo* (*took>toŏk*) (*should> shoŏd*).
4. Short *e* often sounds like short *a* (*nest>nast*) (*bet>bat*).
5. Short *a* usually sounds like short *o* or short *e*. (*apple>ehpple* or *ahpple*), (*sang>sehng* or *sahng*), (*that>thet* or *thaht*).
6. The sound of *ah* or *eh* may be substituted for the sound of *uh* (*up>ahp*) (*sofa>sofah*).

Consonant Sound Substitutions

In English:	In Spanish:	Possible Substitutions:
English has many plosive sounds which require vigorous output of air (*ch, j, zh,* etc.).	In Spanish, the air flow is low. Voiceless sounds are often substituted for the English counterparts.	chair>shair watches>washes match>mash orange>orntch
English words end in at least forty different phonemes.	Only ten main sounds are heard at the end of words, *a, e, i, o, u, l, r, n, s,* and *d*.	eyes>ice bug>buk time>tine want>wahn
th is an unvoiced continuant sound.	No unvoiced *th* sound exists.	this>dis breathless>breafless or breatless both>bof or bot
sh is a voiceless continuant.	No *sh* sound exists.	shoes>chooss fishing>fitching wish>witch
j is a plosive sound requiring high output of air.	No *j* sound exists, closest approximation is *ll* (yellow) or *y* (year).	jump>yump cage>caych
s is given the voiced *z* sound at the end of many words.	No words end in *z* sound.	freeze>freess roses>rossess pleasure>plesher

Grammatical Structures

In English:	In Spanish:	Possible Substitutions:
Word order pattern is *adjective, noun, verb*.	Word order pattern is *noun, adjective*.	"I ate a crisp juicy apple," becomes, "I ate an apple, crisp and juicy."

Grammatical Structures

In English:	In Spanish:	Possible Substitutions:
Linking verbs are used to denote tense change.	Most verb are inflectionalized. Linking verbs not used.	She is working>She working I'm not working>I not working I will do my work later>I work later
Change of word order is made to transform a statement to a question. (He works.>Does he work?)	Question transforms are achieved through voice inflection.	He works.>He works? This is Tuesday. This is Tuesday?

INTERFERENCE PROBLEMS—WHEN THERE IS DIALECTICAL DIFFERENCE

Reading is often defined as talk written down. Granted, print is the symbolic form of oral speech, but it is not necessarily a replication of common usage speech. The more formalized and elaborate structures of printed materials found in textbooks rarely represent childhood conversation.

Under ordinary circumstances, however, the reader converts the more formalized linguistic structures to his own linguistic pattern. Shuy[4] refers to this as an editing process as we "input through a recognition vocabulary and output through a common usage vocabulary." Just as you would "output" through common usage English your interpretation of something written in Elizabethan English, so do most children convert standard formalized English to their own linguistic system. The question is, "When does the dialect difference become a barrier to reading success?"

Whether dialect interferes with the reading process depends upon the degree to which the child's linguistic pattern differs from standard

---

[4]Roger W. Shuy, "Speech Differences and Teaching Strategies: How Different is Enough?" in *Language and Learning to Read,* ed. Richard E. Hodges and E. Hugh Rudolph (Boston: Houghton Mifflin Company, 1972.)

English and the methods and materials used in beginning reading. More specifically, dialect can make a difference:

1. if grammatical forms differ to the degree that the child loses interest before he is able to convert the new language system to his own linguistic pattern;
2. if phonological elements differ to the degree that the child is unable to decode printed forms to words he knows;
3. if the speech of the teacher or peers differs to the degree that the child is unable or unwilling to communicate;
4. if the child is pressured into dealing with printed forms that he has not heard or spoken.

It is safe to say that dialect difference poses a potential problem to a child's success in reading unless the teacher understands the nature of the difference and then modifies reading instruction to deal with that difference.

Regional Versus Social Class Dialects

Regional dialects as found in distinctive geographic areas of the United States are ordinarily reflected in phonological features of the language rather than in grammatical forms. Whether *vigor* is pronounced as *vigah,* *here* as *heah,* or *aunt* as *ant,* appears to be of less social significance than difference in grammatical forms.

Dialect reflecting grammatical irregularities is not so readily accepted. "He bes gone," as compared to "He is gone" or "We was going," as compared to "We were going" carries a social stigma that invites ridicule and suggests social stratification. For whatever reason, it is the latter that constitutes greater interference in the reading process. Rarely does a Texas drawl or a New England accent interfere with a child's ability to read, but there is reason to think that grammatical differences do account for many problems.

Black Dialect as a Language System

Although there is among Blacks, as in any ethnic group, a social stratification reflecting a lower socioeconomic level, a middle class level, and an upper socioeconomic level, linguists contend that American Blacks have developed a separate, well-defined language with a unique and systematized grammatical pattern. Although more commonly used by the lower socioeconomic groups, it is a fully formed linguistic system found throughout the United States. Some of those forms are reflected in the following chart:

WHEN SPEECH REFLECTS A SOCIAL DIALECT

CONTRASTS BETWEEN BLACK DIALECT
AND STANDARD ENGLISH

Grammatical Patterns

Standard English	Black dialect	The Deviation
She goes to school. He doesn't swim.	She go to school. He don't swim.	The *s* ending is not used in the verb system.
He comes to work at eight. He came at seven yesterday.	He come to work at eight. He come at seven yesterday.	Some irregular verbs have the same form for present or past tense.
She walked to school. She missed the bus yesterday.	She walk to school. She had miss the bus yesterday.	The *ed* ending is not used to form past tense.
I've been away. She's been ill.	I been away. She been ill.	The contractions *have* and *has* are often dropped.
I take Algebra. I took Algebra. I have taken Algebra.	I take Algebra. I have took Algebra. I taken Algebra.	Conjugation of verb "to take" reverses use of *have.*
I do my work. I did my work. I have done my work.	I do my work. I done my work. I have did my work.	Conjugation of verb "to do" reverses using *have.*
She is talking. She is talking.	She be talking. (at the moment) She bes talking. (habitually, she is)	Verb "to be" takes on shades of meaning.

Phonological Patterns

Black Dialect	Substitutions
The th problem:	
this>dis	voiced *th* in initial position becomes *d.*

Phonological Patterns

Black Dialect	Substitutions
breathe>breave	voice *th* in final position becomes *v*.
mother>muvver	voiced *th* in medial position becomes *v* or *t*.
south>souf	unvoiced *th* in final position becomes *f*.

The r problem:

car>cah	*r* sound is slurred or omitted
floor>flow or flaw	(creates many homonyms).
starter>stahter	
sugar>shugah	
tire>tah	

CONCLUSIONS AND IMPLICATIONS

In order for children to code symbols to speech they must (1) hear the sound, (2) be able to reproduce the sound, and (3) associate the sound with the corresponding letter symbol. This approach implies that teachers must:

1. Listen to the student's speech and analyze the contrasts between his speech and standard English.
2. Introduce alternate patterns.
3. Provide a language-saturated environment that permits a child to practice standard English in a functional setting.
4. Plan a systematic introduction of English sounds and structures built on a simple rationale:
   Listen (the teacher models)
   Listen and Say (child repeats)
   Say and Look (teacher models and writes)
   Look, Read and Build (child repeats, reads, produces another word that has the same sound or sounds)

EXTENDED READINGS

Baratz, Joan C., and Roger W. Shuy, eds. *Teaching Black Children to Read.* Washington, D.C.: Center for Applied Linguistics, 1969.

Bordie, John G. "When Should Instruction in a Second Language or Dialect Begin?" *Elementary English* 48 (May 1971):551–54.

Brown, Roger and Ursula Bellugi. "Three Processes in the Child's Acquisition of Syntax." *Harvard Educational Review* 34 (Spring 1964):133–151.

Ching, Doris. "Reading, Language Development, and the Bilingual Child," *Elementary English* (May 1969).

Eisenhardt, Catheryn. *Applying Linguistics in the Teaching of Reading and Language Arts.* Columbus, Ohio: Charles E. Merrill Publishing Company, 1972, pp. 13–25.

Gladney, Mildred R. and Lloyd Leaverton. "A Model for Teaching Standard English to Non-Standard English Speakers." *Elementary English* 1968: 758–763.

Heilman, Arthur W. *Principles and Practices of Teaching Reading,* Third Edition. Columbus, Ohio: Charles E. Merrill Publishing Company, 1972, pp. 23–99.

Johnson, Kenneth R. "Teachers Attitude Toward the Non-Standard Negro Dialect." *Elementary English* 48 (February 1971):176–182.

————— "False Assumptions Teachers Make about Non-Standard Negro Dialect." Paper presented at the T.E.S.O.L. Convention, San Francisco, March 1970.

Loban, Walter D. *The Language of Elementary School Children.* Champaign, Ill., N.C.T.E. Research Report number one, 1963.

Labov, William. *The Study of Non-Standard English.* Washington, D.C.: Center for Applied Linguistics, 1969. Available from National Council of Teachers of English, Urbana, Illinois.

Marquardt, William F. "Language Interference in Reading." *The Reading Teacher* 18 (December 1964):214–218.

McDavid, Raven I., Jr. *American Social Dialects.* Champaign, Ill.: N.C.T.E., 1955.

Olguin, Leonard. *Shuck Loves Chirley.* Original American Press, distributed by A. C. Vronan, Pasadena, California. (Diagnostic tests and helps for teachers working with Chicano Children.)

Rystrom, Richard. "Dialect Training and Reading: A Further Look." *Reading Research Quarterly* (Summer 1970):581–599.

Smith, Frank. *Understanding Reading: A Psycholinguistic Analysis of Reading and Learning to Read.* New York: Holt, Rinehart and Winston, 1971.

Tireman, Loyd S. *Teaching Spanish-Speaking Children,* Revised ed. University of New Mexico, 1951.

Williamson, Juanita. "A Look at Black English." *The Crisis* 78, no. 6 (1970): 169–173.

Wasserman, Susan. "Raising the English Language Proficiency of Mexican American Children in the Primary Grades." *California English Journal* (April 1970): 22–27.

CHAPTER 4

In the
Tender Years—
Half Past
Babyhood

In the midwest, winters can be bitterly cold. Snow often covers garden spaces long past the time meant for spring planting. I recall vividly my mother's scheme to outwit nature each spring season as she prepared for her early garden. She dug deep into the rich soil on the sunny side of a rolling hill, pulverizing the earth in a plot just the right dimension to be covered by a large wooden window frame, complete with glass panes. This was her miniature hot-house where seeds were carefully planted in small ridges or clumps.

There, protected from cold, in a climate rich, warm, and moist, small brown seeds thrived and quickly grew into seedlings. When the stems were strong enough to withstand the weather, and the roots sturdy enough to draw life from the soil, she carefully transferred them to the large garden where they were ready for sun, winds, and occasional hailstorms.

Early childhood should be like that. Tender things, children too, thrive in a rich, warm emotional climate. Protected, yet nurtured and stimulated while minds and bodies draw strength for growing on their own. What a dream—that all children everywhere might have such a time for growing!

Each September, thousands of five- and six-year-olds troop into classrooms to begin the first step in formal education. Eager or reluctant, advanced or immature, their entry is permitted on the basis of chronological age. The wisdom of disregarding social age and emotional maturity as factors revelant to school entry has long been debated. Since entry age cut-off dates vary from school district to school district, many problems arise in regard to organizational plans and curricular provisions. It is the primary teacher, however, who must cope with this interesting challenge on "Day One" of each new school term.

MEET TONY!

Tony is six years and eleven months of age. He missed the entry date by one month last year. Physically, he is a head taller than many other boys in the class. Although he has not been enrolled in kindergarten, he did participate in a summer Head Start program.

Tony's big black eyes and dark complexion suggest a mixed ethnic background. Although his mother and father speak English, their language reflects a strong social dialect. The grandmother, who lives with the family, speaks only Italian. Tony's speech repertoire is a blend of both. Included are a few choice expressions from older boys in the neighborhood.

Tony is a "mover." He has to touch, feel, push, pull, or manipulate everything in the classroom. His attention span is short. He is the first one to edge away from the group during the story hour, the first one in line at recess, and the only one who simply cannot "remember" to bring something for show and tell period.

Tony's art efforts to date are blobs scrubbed on a paper with a brush dipped in all six bottles of paint. However, his clay model of a car is the "best one" according to his friends. In singing—he would rather not!

If the task is picture matching, putting together a puzzle, or copying designs, Tony is successful. He is well coordinated in eye-hand and eye-foot movement. He likes to work with counting devices and blocks.

Tony's vocabulary is limited to utility words related to the here and now. He squirms out of every situation that requires him to speak in front of a group and he squirms into every situation that offers promise of physical combat.

THIS IS DELIA

Delia's sixth birthday fell two days before the enrollment entry date. She is almost a year younger than many of her classmates. She is the youngest of five children of a Negro family. She has not been enrolled in any type of preschool program.

Delia is a quiet child. She sits close to the teacher. She will listen as long as someone is willing to read. She loves to sing and she remembers melodies. She enjoys poems and rhymes but only as a listener. She tires easily and often retreats with thumb in mouth rather than join in a game or activity. Delia atriculates clearly. She uses full sentence responses. The grammatical structure of her speech is reflected in such patterns as, "Ah is six years ol! She be's my sister. We's goan to the desert."

Delia's hand-eye coordination is not well developed. She has much difficulty in handling a pencil or a brush. She does not enjoy puzzles. She does not discriminate differences or see likenesses in shapes, designs, or details, yet she can sing back a series of musical notes in perfect pitch.

THEN, THERE IS MARIE

Marie is as "unaverage" as any first grade child you'll find. True, she is six years of age, but she is taller than any girl in her class, thinner than most, and more physically aggressive than all put together! She is impulsive, vigorous, and domineering.

Marie is one of seven children, third in line. She competes (quite successfully) with four younger brothers and is tolerated by two older sisters. Her family lives in crowded quarters. The noise level of the busy household is consistent with the ever-present clang and clatter of the busy street a few feet from the door.

Marie has adapted to the situation as she found it. She acts first and then explains if it's necessary. She gets what she wants with as little communication as possible. She deals in realities. Instant gratification has become a life style.

In the classroom, Marie exhibits sheer agony if confined to a desk. While she can overpower and outwit any of her peers physically, her energies relate more to survival tactics. She has not developed manipulative skills and this is apparent in pencil and paper tasks as well as playground games involving specific motor skills. Furthermore, she reaches a low energy level about midmorning. She appears to expend her energy in impulsive behavior, leaving little for classroom learning tasks.

At home, verbal communication is limited to basic needs and concerns. Her mother does housework and ironing "on the outside" to supplement funds. Consequently, the children fend for themselves much of the time. Marie's vocabulary is adequate for outside school needs, but is woefully limited for in-school tasks.

No one can say that Marie lacks experiences or language. It just happens that her frame of reference is different from the school-related tasks, and her speech, though entirely functional (for her), differs dramatically from the language context of books found in her classroom.

Tony, Delia and Marie are only three members of a class of thirty students in a school situated in an economically depressed school community. Enrollees represent a wide range of preschool experience and highly divergent linguistic systems.

Seven speak Spanish by preference, understand English, but use it only when necessary. Only two are functionally fluent in both English and Spanish. Seven use "conventionalized" dialectical speech characterized as non-standard English. One is fluent as a bilingual in English and Japanese. Remaining enrollees are English-speaking monolinguals.

Four of the class members have spent two years in day care centers. Ten were enrolled in a Head Start program for a full year. Five had participated in a summer Head Start program. Two were enrolled the previous term in public school kindergarten and five have never been enrolled in any type of preschool program.

Three of the students are Indian children living in foster homes during the school term. Both parents of fifty percent of the class work during daytime hours. Ten of the families represented are welfare recipients.

The diversity described typifies many school situations in the United States. The questions are:

1. What levels of social, emotional and linguistic development would you expect to find among the students of this class?
2. What is the relationship among chronological age, mental age, and psycho-social age?
3. In view of the divergence of background among these students, what is the role of the teacher?
4. What objectives should be set for the year's program in view of the wide range of school readiness among the students?
5. What organizational plan can the school provide to assure that each student will progress at his maximum potential?
6. What predictions would you make concerning some priorities in instruction?

FROM THE OUTSIDE SCHOOL TO THE INSIDE SCHOOL

He Takes a Giant Step

The young child entering school for the first time crosses a threshold wider than any he is ever again to experience. With one hand yet holding fast to the security of home and parent and the other stretched inquisitively toward an unknown world called school, he is as sensitive as a violin string, as unpredictable as the north wind, and as pliable as a piece of warm clay. A teacher of beginning students is charged with a precious task, for this is a time when egos are easily bruised, and habits are quickly formed. Life styles in learning probably are shaped during this critical period.

Change in routine, longer periods of inaction, association with a group, and separation from parents or siblings make first days in school a period of stress for some children. The wider the gap between the home environment and the school environment, the more difficult is the transition. Add to the normal differences between home and school a language that is different, customs that are different, and a way of dress that may be unlike that of other class members, and it is easy to understand why many children from foreign language backgrounds or from underprivileged homes seek out dark corners of the classroom with thumb in mouth. Dropout candidates probably begin their retreat in the first two or three years of school and simply continue backing away until they fade from sight as soon as age or law allows.

Sylvia Ashton Warner, a former teacher of Maori children in New Zealand, states in her book, *Teacher:*

> At a tender age a wrench occurs from one culture to another, from which either manifestly or subconsciously not all recover. And I think that this circumstance has some little bearing on the number of Maoris who, although well-educated, seem neurotic, and on the number who retreat to the mat.[1]

It is no secret that a high percentage of high school dropouts come from bicultural backgrounds.

He Needs Time to Discover His New World

The young child entering school handicapped by differences of any kind needs time to grow into the new patterns, time to overcome his fears and anxieties, time to listen, touch, feel, and sense the newness before he is pushed into tasks that may be beyond his stage of development and his scope of experience. If teachers can only resist the passion to gain time with the beginning student, there is a chance that the wrench from one culture to another many not occur. It is not the pages covered in a book

---

[1]Sylvia Ashton Warner, *Teacher* (New York: Simon and Schuster, 1963), p. 28.

nor the number of workbooks completed that determine progress. (After all, language is not imprisoned between the covers of a book.) Reading is speech *pictured, printed,* and *preserved* on paper. A child is not ready to deal with the secondary form of speech before he deals with the primary form.

Long before reading and writing there is talk:

> Listening and telling, sharing and asking, conversations and discussion—*words, words,* and more *words,*
> pictures and films, things to touch, to feel, to explore—*experiences, experiences,* and more *experiences,*
> rhymes and rhythms, sounds and movements—*activities, activities,* and more *activities,*
> bugs and beetles, fishes and frogs, plants and seeds and all the *things that grow and breathe,*
> wheels and levers, trucks and trains, and all the things that move and fly and float—*discovery, discovery,* and more *discovery.*

The four walls of a classroom were never meant to shut out the world outside but only to corral for a time the charging power of children's minds. In the creative classroom, where ideas are born and nursed to maturity, teachers need only harness that power and head it in the right direction. Quoting again from Sylvia Ashton Warner, "The expansion of a child's mind can be beautiful growth. And in beauty are included the qualities of equilibrium, harmony and rest." And then she adds, "I can't disassociate the activity in an infant room from war and peace. So often I have seen the destructive vent, beneath an onslaught of creativity, dry up under my eyes."[2]

Child of Five is a Word Collector

The five-year-old is an adventurer. He collects things! Among his treasures there may be beetles, bugs, badges, buckles, and bottle caps. Words, too, are a part of this assorted collection. Normally by the time he enters school, he has accumulated a vocabulary commensurate with his communicative needs. There may be long words, short words, weed-patch-variety words, slightly bent "sophisticated" grown-up words, delightfully descriptive original words—no matter, they all come tumbling out like marbles from a bag. Some are "puries," some earthly clay, and some as shining as agate. They may be scattered, scrambled, or lined

---

up in orderly rows, but eventually they fall into colorful, satisfying patterns of speech called childhood conversation—in English, in French, in Spanish, in Navajo or any other language.

His utterances are an outgrowth of all the concepts he has accumulated. In no measure, however, does he possess the verbal facility to express all the ideas or the knowledge he has acquired. His experience in nonverbal communication compensates in part for verbal limitations, and at times may serve more powerfully than words.

He Has A Dual Vocabulary

The words the child uses in speech represent only a part of his total vocabulary. The words a child understands but is unable or unwilling to use represent the other part. There is no logical way to estimate the meaning vocabulary of the young child since this relates more to contextual references than actual words. Children follow the flow of ideas in adult conversations without actually knowing the meaning of many of the words used. The recognition vocabulary floats just below the surface of the child's speaking vocabulary, emerging gradually to join the stream of functional speech as the child matures.

His Vocabulary Can Be Classified

Listen to the five year old! He makes language work for him. He manipulates words to serve two major purposes:

1. *to name things and describe them:* big horse, little cat, this red book, in English; *caballo grande* (horse, large), *gato pequeno* (cat, small), *este libro rojo* (this book, red) in Spanish.

2. *to express action and qualify that action:* run fast, come here, in English; *corre muy rápida* (run very fast) in Spanish.

All other words serve in one way or another to specify conditions, to connect endless streams of conversations or to express feelings or emotions. Later, teachers will tack titles such as nouns, adjectives, adverbs, conjunctions, determiners, auxiliaries, and subordinators to his words, but in the functional scheme of childhood language, rules have little to do with vocabulary acquisition.

He Is Egocentric

At five and six years of age, the child is yet a self-centered being who can be very aggressive in his desire to be seen and heard. If he fails to receive the attention he wants, he may resort to a number of options; he may compensate for his ego needs by creating distractions and disturbances, by clowning, by feigning illness or pain, by resorting to another area of interest, or by withdrawing from the scene altogether.

Maslow's studies emphasize the importance of psychological needs in the development of personality. Unless the individual's needs for self-esteem and self-actualization are met in some measure, he is not likely to be motivated toward the higher order of wants—the need to know and to understand.[3] Those self-actualizing needs are acute during the egocentric stage of development.

The drive for self-actualization can be a powerful force in launching children into a successful beginning in reading or it can be reason for a slow and discouraging reading experience.

When there is "will and wanting," students appear to be able to learn to read in spite of handicaps, social disadvantages, and physical disabilities. Partially-sighted students often manage to become adept and productive readers. Socially disadvantaged students can become avid readers in spite of the fact that their own experiences may be extremely divergent from the context of materials employed for instruction. Conversely, it can happen that a student who is physically fit, mentally bright, socially well-adjusted and appears to have been advantaged by an affluent home situation fails to become a successful reader. Although there are countless reasons for reading failure, attitude and desire to read appear to be the most significant reasons for reading success.

CAPITALIZING ON CHARACTERISTICS

If we believe that self-motivation is an important factor in reading success, then the criteria for judging the quality of any program must take into consideration the characteristics of the student. Although each child is a unique being, all children appear to exhibit certain behavioral patterns at particular age levels. Through first hand experience, we have discovered some things about five- and six-year-old children that should serve as criteria for planning reading strategies:

1. They are better "doers" than listeners.
2. They are better "movers" than "sitters."
3. They learn more quickly from first-hand experience.
4. They grasp ideas more readily when they make their own discoveries.

---

[3]A. H. Maslow, "A Theory of Human Motivation," *Psychological Review* 50 (1943): 370–396.

5. They are more concerned about things that relate to their own personal needs.
6. They tend to pursue, with vigor, those activities in which they are successful and resist, with passion, those activities which result in frustration.
7. They perceive new ideas and concepts through the "binoculars of their own experience."

TIME TO GROW TOWARD LANGUAGE POWER

Language power, social emotional growth, and perceptual development are vital components of the reading process. Until the various "publics"—parents, taxpayers, school boards and the public press—accept that idea, the language-different, culture-different student will continue to be a candidate for costly remedial programs.

Some children need much time to develop language power before they are forced into the formal phases of reading symbols. Whether the school provides a kindergarten or not, the first year of the child's school experience should be focused on those strategies that sharpen visual and auditory acuity, extend the functional speaking vocabulary, broaden concepts, and enable the child to function comfortably in a group situation.

Accountability for reading proficiency among language-different students appears to be a shared responsibility. Parents and teachers must agree that the program of oral language development is prerequisite to the reading program and holds high priority as an objective of the primary curriculum. There must be equal recognition and concern for speech development as a goal rather than merely a readiness activity for reading. This point of view suggests that parents and the entire school staff are accountable, and that they share this accountability by supporting some basic ideas about language:

1. Language changes come slowly.
2. Speaking fluency holds high priority in the instructional program.
3. Oral language training must continue throughout the elementary grades for all students, but particularly for bicultural, bilingual students.
4. The bilingual's first language should be used as the bridge to the second language.
5. The student must be assisted in becoming a true bilingual by utilizing both the native tongue and the target language.

Flexible Organization

If the primary program can be regarded as a period of time extending from one to four years, rather than a series of locked-in grade levels, students can progress from one level to another according to their ability. It means the plotting of an organizational plan to maximize the student's opportunity to profit from both his peers and his instructors as he moves along a continuum bumping his head against the ceiling of his own mental-emotional potential.

In such a plan, kindergarten is regarded as a year for rich personal, social, conceptual growth. It is a time for sharpening visual acuity of shapes, forms, and configurations; a time to sensitize auditory awareness of sounds and the rhythm of language; a time to build relationships, of time, of space, of cause and effect. Particularly, it is a time to build a fund of concepts along with the language facility to communicate ideas in relation to those concepts.

DESIGNING FOR DIFFERENTIATION

There have been countless plans devised to organize classroom instruction in order to provide for individual differences among students. The plans range from the formal, traditional grade level organization with a pass-fail concept, to the open-classroom, unstructured, ungraded concept. Such organizational plans are as old as education itself, yet as new as day after tomorrow. It is possible even today to find classrooms where twenty or thirty students are reading from the same reading text, on the same page, at the same moment, regardless of the students' ability range, just as it was fifty years ago. And fifty years ago, it was not unheard of to have students gathered into small clusters working at ability level; in fact, the open classroom, multilevel curricular organizational plan, grades one through eight, complete with partner learning and the "buddy system" probably was first conceived (if not by design by necessity) in rural school rooms where one teacher was responsible for thirty-five to forty students ranging in age from six to sixteen. While the motive may have been survival, the tactics might easily be regarded as innovative!

Approaches to Differentiated Instruction

Although many different organizational plans have been initiated to differentiate instruction, the strategies can be narrowed down to three rather distinctive approaches, as illustrated in the chart below.

Grade Level Instruction	Ability Group Instruction	Individualized Instruction
Student is instructed in grade level class with no provisions for individual difference.	Student is assigned to designated ability group according to assessed level of ability.	Student works individually within a self-pacing concept.
Pre-determined grade level expectations held for all students.	Materials and instruction are geared to the group level.	Instruction is carried out through teacher-student conference periods.
Pass-fail policy is on grade level criterion.	Student progresses from group to group according to demonstrated ability at each level.	Materials of instruction are geared to each student's instructional level.
		Student progresses at his own ability level.

Obviously, the first strategy makes little or no provision for individual difference. The "sink or swim" concept is based upon a grade level criterion that all students are expected to reach.

The second strategy, based on the concept of homogeneity, makes some provision for individual difference by limiting the range of ability within the group. Thus a teacher would "cluster" a small number of students for reading instruction. Feasibly, there might be three or four different reading groups within the class, each at a different instructional level. While this provides for a more limited range than the "one-grade-one-group-one-book" plan, any teacher will tell you that each group could be sub-grouped. No student is likely to have his individual needs fully met in the group situation.

The third strategy, individualized instruction, is based on Olsen's principles of self-seeking, self-selection, and self-pacing. Concern in this strategy is placed on personal involvement and individual interest. The strategy is designed to provide a one-to-one relationship with the instructor, which theoretically will permit each student to progress at his own rate and ability level. Heilman[4] points out some limitations of the approach, stating that the success or failure of individualized instruction rests almost exclusively with the teacher. Individualizing instruction requires much time and effort not only in securing materials and programming individual activities, but in holding individual student con-

---

[4]Arthur W. Heilman, *Principles and Practices of Teaching Reading,* 3rd ed. (Columbus, Ohio: Charles E. Merrill Publishing Co., 1972), p. 390.

ferences as well. The principles of individualized instruction are sound. The limitations relate to the expertise of the teacher in meeting the demands of each student, and in budgeting time to insure that all students are given adequate guidance.

Structure Versus Unstructure

The pendulum swings from time to time from one extreme to another. Currently, many schools, particularly at primary levels, have swung in the direction of individualized instruction in an open-classroom situation where a team of three or four teachers may work with sixty to one hundred students in a somewhat unstructured approach. Reading instruction is carried out either in ability groups directed by different members of the team, or through the individualized approach.

The trend toward the unstructured approach has brought criticism from those who fear that fundamentals and skill instruction will become incidental and that some students will be lost in the shuffle of informality. Proponents contend that students must be broken out of the "lock-step, grade level designation," if they are ever to become self-learners.

It would be impossible to enumerate or describe the varied strategies found in current practices. We can, however, examine three types of organization in an effort to pinpoint some of the advantages and limitations of each type that are frequently cited by classroom teachers (see p. 55).

The question is not which plan is best, but which plan is best under the particular circumstances. Obviously, no plan is without limitations, and no plan is unworthy if it is working.

Some teachers have found that they can work out plans for crossing grade lines in order to "cluster" children for reading instruction. Some teachers are able to manage in-class groupings and carry out an individualized reading program by planning individual conferences with each student. Other teachers have been able to carry out a completely individualized reading program in a self-contained classroom.

The criterion for success of any strategy for classroom organization rests upon the total effort of the school staff in agreeing upon objectives and setting up strategies and organizational designs to carry out those objectives.

NOT A QUESTION OF "EITHER-OR"

Piaget[5] stresses two basic premises in his philosophy of education. First, that the child is the principal agent in his own educational develop-

---

[5] Evelyn Lawrence, T. R. Theakston, and N. Isaacs, *Some Aspects of Piaget's Work* (London: National Froebel Foundation, 1957).

A COMPARISON OF THREE TYPES OF ORGANIZATION PLANS FOR CLASSROOM INSTRUCTION

	Advantages	*Demands*
Self-Contained Classroom *One Teacher Instruction*	1. Continuity of instruction. 2. Integration of subject matter. 3. Flexibility of time. 4. Opportunity for follow-through in all areas.	1. Time to meet individual needs. 2. Accountability for all areas of curriculum. 3. Management problems related to classroom control, supervision of individual work, and evaluation of each child's progress.
Self-Contained Classroom *Students deployed for cross-grade or cross-level ability instruction in reading*	1. Narrows the range of individual difference. 2. Provides more time for individual needs. 3. Capitalizes on expertise of staff members. 4. Accountability for pupil progress is shared by two or more instructors.	1. Isolates reading instruction from other areas of the curriculum. 2. Evaluation usually based upon performance or special reading period, rather than on total reading performance in areas of application. 3. Non-flexible time period.
Open Classroom Multi-level Grouping *Team Instruction*	1. Permits small group instruction in a multilevel setting. 2. Allows for continuity of instruction. 3. Capitalizes on total team expertise in planning, instructing, and evaluating. 4. Permits flexible scheduling. 5. Maximizes opportunity for continuous stranding as opposed to grade level assignment. 6. Accountability for total instruction is shared by a teaching team.	1. Requires total team effort and agreement on philosophy. 2. Necessitates close working relationship of total staff. 3. Roles of team members must be agreed upon and clearly established. 4. Necessitates much time for team planning. 5. Requires high level organization to assure that each student's needs are met.

ment. His path to understanding is unlike that of any other child. At the same time, he suggests that when the individual sees the world from only his own point of view, he imprisons himself. This leads to Piaget's second premise in which he holds that it is through interaction with a peer group that the child is drawn out of his egocentrism. By testing his ideas with others, he develops objectivity and moves toward rationality. The importance of group dynamics in relation to planning, sharing, comparing and decision-making is as crucially important in the classroom in terms of broadening the students' perspectives.

Based on this point of view, children need both the structured group experience where group interaction is facilitated by the teacher and unstructured individual learning experiences through which each child moves along his own individual track. Such organization must provide a balance of:

1. structured, teacher-directed activities
2. semi-structured, teacher-guided activities
3. directed, individualized activities
4. self-directed, self-selected activities

A BALANCED PLAN OF ACTION

A best-of-two-worlds approach would be to capitalize on the strengths of structured group organization, ability grouping, and individualized instruction. Such a plan would provide for:

1. Large group activities designed to involve the total class in idea sharing, problem solving, and verbal interaction.
2. Small group activities designed to direct or guide small groups of students in specific areas according to ability or interest level.
3. Individualized activity designed to provide one-to-one relationship between a pupil and the instructor.
4. Learning Center activities designed to extend, to reinforce, and to enrich regular classroom instruction through self-directed learning experiences.

The chart on page 57 is intended to show how the classroom might be organized to implement the activity-centered plan. It is adaptable to a single teacher classroom, as well as to an open classroom with a team of teachers. Logically, the plan can be carried out more easily in team teaching where instructional tasks, group guidance, and individual con-

A SUGGESTED PROGRAM FOR EARLY PRIMARY LEVELS

Structured Activities	Semi-Structured Activities	Unstructured Activities
Large Group	*Large Group*	*Large Group*
Planning time; Teacher-directed discussion of:	Total class working on such projects as:	Sharing time period provided for:
1. plans for the day	1. social living unit activities (charts, displays, talking murals, bulletin boards, in-door out-door construction projects, experience charts)	1. show and tell experience
2. classroom goals		2. reporting on individual or group activities
3. preparation for class projects, field trips, social activities, etc.	2. science activities, (collections, labeled displays, experience charts, records of experiments, in-door out-door gardens, science word dictionaries or files)	3. showing art work, reading creative stories, poems, etc. Library period set aside for independent reading or "picture reading" listening to "talking books" etc.
4. classroom rules and regulations		
5. housekeeping task assignments	3. a classroom newspaper or news sheet	
Small Group	4. Literary experiences, story reading, story telling, poetry, recordings, creative writing	Demonstration period provided for:
Ability group instruction in beginning language and reading	5. Creative dramatics	1. creative dramatic presentations
1. oral language		2. puppet shows
2. vocabulary building		3. individual talent opportunity
3. visual and auditory skill building activities		4. choral reading
4. concept building	*Small Group*	*Small Group*
5. language experience activity	Groups "cycled" through learning centers for specific learning experiences:	Clusters of children involved in cooperative work or play activity
Individual	1. Library Center	*Individual*
Teacher directed individual learning experiences such as:	2. Listening-viewing Station	Free-choice activity in learning center. Play-house area, toy or game area, art or crafts area, etc.
1. programmed instruction in silent reading, and perceptual skill development	3. Reading Skills Center (games and manipulative devices)	
2. Teacher-constructed tapes and work sheets.	4. Creative Writing Center	Individual choice work tasks related to plans of the day.
	5. Science Center	
	Individual	
	Individuals assigned to learning centers for specific learning experiences	

ferencing could be programmed simultaneously since each member of the instructional team can function in a different area.

Above all else, the needs of the culture-different, language-different student can be met only when there is maximum provision for one-to-one relationship between child and instructor. Hopefully, the total staff of any school will dedicate its efforts toward this goal.

The possibilities for differentiated instruction can be explored by "experimenting" with the following schematic design. Assume that the team consists of two certified teachers, a para-professional aide, a parent or volunteer aide, and perhaps a student teacher.

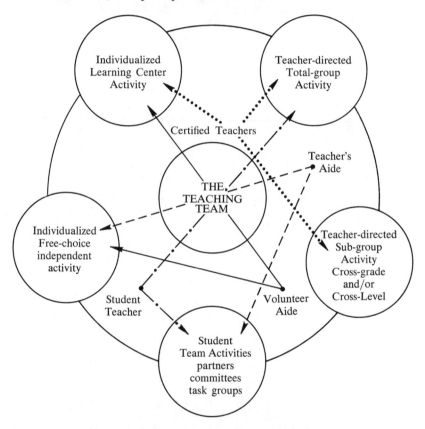

1. How do you perceive the role of each team member?
2. Consider the various ways the team might work together.
3. Picture the possibilities for individualizing instruction in this plan.

4. Switch arrows to show how each team member might function in another role.

EXTENDED READINGS

Blakely, W. Paul, and Emma M. Shadle. "A Study of Two Readiness-for-Reading Programs in Kindergarten." *Elementary English* (November 1961): 502–6.

Chilman, Catherine S. "Some Angles on Parent-Teacher Learning." *Childhood Education* 48, no. 3 (December 1971):119–125.

Chukovsky, Kornei. *From Two to Five*. Berkeley: University of California Press, 1968.

Church, Joseph. "Language in Childhood." Washington D.C.: A.C.E.I. Readings from *Childhood Education,* 1966, pp. 223–226.

Hymes, James L. *Before a Child Reads*. New York: Harper and Row, 1958.

Ilg, Frances L. and Louise B. Ames. *School Readiness*. New York: Harper and Row, 1964.

Irwin, O. C. "Infant speech: the effect of family occupational status and of age on sound frequency." *Journal of Speech and Hearing Disorders* 13 (1948): 320–323.

James, Elizabeth. "Involving Parents in Children's Learning." *Childhood Education* 47, no. 3 (December 1970):126–130.

Miller, Wilma H. *Elementary Reading Today: Selected Articles*. New York: Holt, Rinehart and Winston, Inc. Chapter 4: The Home Environment of Culturally Disadvantaged Children. Chapter 5: Early Blocks to Children's Learning.

McCarthy, Dorothea. *Language Development of the Pre-School Child*. Inst. Child Welfare Monograph No. 4. Minneapolis, 1930.

Washburne, Carlton. "Ripeness." *Progressive Education* XIII (February 1936): 125–130.

Beginning
Steps

Work Skills: Demonstrates ability to carry out purposeful learning activities.

Visual Perception: Perceives similarities and differences in letter symbols and word shapes. Coordinates eye-movement. Demonstrates sense of directionality.

Auditory Perception: Demonstrates ability to hear similarities and differences in speech sounds and in words.

Conceptual Relationship Understandings: Demonstrates a general grasp of *time, place, size,* and *quantity* relationships. Can verbalize thoughts in organized sequence.

Perceptual Motor Abilities: Demonstrates muscular coordination in manipulation of games, toys and tools of instruction, handling books, pictures, and similar types of printed material, and coping with near-point visual tasks.

Speaking Facility: Demonstrates ability to communicate needs, responds to questions, and converses with classmates, in English, using sentence structures rather than one word responses or gestures.

Auditory Functioning: Sustains attention long enough to profit from appropriate directed instruction. Demonstrates response to rhyme and rhythms of English language. Responds to oral directives.

Reading is a process of building on to the psychomotor skills and communication abilities that have been acquired through early childhood experiences. While there is no rigid sequence in the level of these behaviors and abilities, each phase of development represents a foundational step toward the more precise abilities required in the reading act.

The instructional program begins by strengthening the modalities through which the child learns. Input comes first. Language facility develops as an integral part of the sensorimotor experiences. As the child manipulates the toys and tools of his beginning primary experiences, he develops finer motor coordination. As he invents and discovers through problem-solving situations, he begins to develop differential perceptual abilities, both auditory and visual. As he works in a group environment where verbal interaction is a part of the action, language meanings and verbal facility develop on a functional level.

Cognitive Development

We know very little about how a child thinks. We can only observe and hypothesize. Piaget's description of mental organization has been widely accepted. According to this theory, at birth the infant has no specific knowledge, but is innately equipped to organize and adapt sensory information. Through the senses of sight, hearing, taste, touch and smell there is constant input of information which is adapted through a process of assimilation and accommodation. In other words, continuous restructuring takes place as incoming information adds to, changes, or modifies whatever perceptual and conceptual knowledge exists in the mind.[1]

It is Piaget's contention that stages of mental organization occur in the same sequence for all individuals though the rate at which a child moves through the sequence may differ. The process has little to do with chronological age.

Training, to be effective, must parallel these stages of cognitive development. If the child is pushed into tasks beyond his mental functioning level, he is prevented from "discovering for himself." On the other hand, the mental operation process is continuous. There is constant sensory input of one type or another every waking moment. The mind can process only that which is channeled to it. (This should dispel any notion that reading readiness is a waiting period.)

---

[1]John H. Flavell, *The Developmental Psychology of Jean Piaget* (New York: Van Nostrand, 1963). Flavel's interpretation of Piaget's contributions is directed to the classroom teacher. It should be read in detail.

Input, Output Processes

Based on this theory, it is possible to construct a schema (Page 64) that suggests a relationship between intellectual functioning and the communicative process. We might view the receptive processes as sensory input. In turn input is processed, assimilated, accommodated, and stored for retrieval. Perceived in this way, the type and quality of sensory information channeled into the mental processing operation directly affects the "output," or the expressive phases.

Factors That Interfere with the Process

It is evident that the relationship of language and learning is complex. The entire process is dependent upon the type and quality of sensory information received, but is also subject to countless factors that bombard the system with interference. Just as a computer can be jammed with confusing information or disabled because of operational difficulties, so can mental functioning be affected by a multiplicity of environmental factors.

Physical limitations, mental age, emotional problems, and negative attitudes may jam up, slow down, or limit the functioning. Lack of intellectual stimulation, deprivation, and a host of other environmental factors can interfere with the cognitive process. Furthermore there is little doubt that children differ in the mode or manner through which they learn best. Whether viewed as a consequence of innate tendencies or environmental influence, some children appear to learn more readily through auditory channels, others through visual channels, and still others through a combination of visual-tactile-auditory experiences.

THE FIRST STEP—ASSESSMENT

Assessment and instruction go hand in hand and the process is continuous. Identifying a child's stage of development as he enters school is important in terms of assessing immediate physical and psycho-social needs, and in terms of setting up objectives for his educational program.

Many skills requisite to success in reading are predictable and identifiable. Before objectives can be set up for the reading readiness program, there must be individual assessment of development in regard to the child's (1) *listening comprehension,* (2) *attention span,* (3) *motor-coordination,* (4) *auditory discrimination,* (5) *speech fluency,* (6) *language concepts,* and (7) *oral vocabulary.*

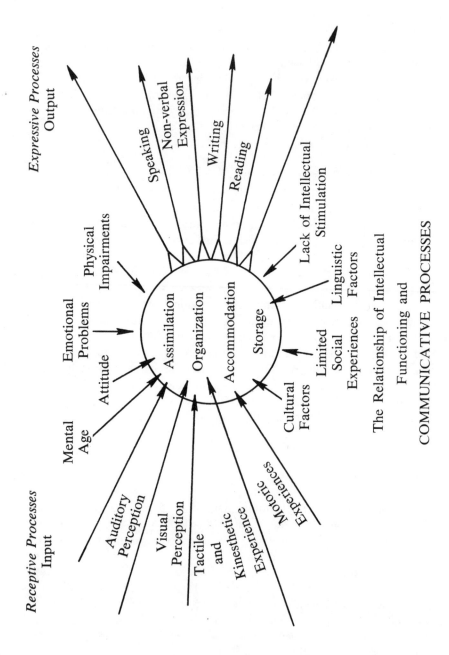

Receptive Processes
Input

Expressive Processes
Output

Speaking
Non-verbal Expression
Writing
Reading

Physical Impairments
Emotional Problems
Attitude
Mental Age
Auditory Perception
Visual Perception
Tactile and Kinesthetic Experience
Motoric Experiences

Assimilation
Organization
Accommodation
Storage

Lack of Intellectual Stimulation
Linguistic Factors
Limited Social Experiences
Cultural Factors

The Relationship of Intellectual
Functioning and
COMMUNICATIVE PROCESSES

64

There is little reason to suppose that any two children will demonstrate the same level of ability in sensorimotor abilities or in language. Testing to determine by which modality a child functions best and to discover the strengths and the limitations can yield information basic to beginning instruction.

Why We Need a Systematic Plan

An organized system of assessment not only saves time but provides a more reliable means of collecting information on a child's level of development. Files need to be set up and kept current on each child. Cumulative records of progress include all results of testing along with anecdotal notations and samples of the child's work from time to time. Such a file provides for continuous assessment of progress.

The chart on page 66 is one means of setting up individual profiles. By assessing levels of development in the eight categories of reading-related behaviors, it is possible to determine strengths and needs. While there is considerable risk in attaching scores to performance levels, categories indicating levels ranging from *advanced* to *very limited* can be used as indicators of a child's readiness to deal with reading tasks.

By charting a child's performance in each of the eight areas listed it is possible to predict immediate needs. For example, a child performing at a very limited stage of development in listening comprehension may be unable to follow verbal directions, while another at an advanced stage of development might be able to listen to an entire story, then re-tell it, in logical sequence in his own words. It can be predicted that the first child mentioned will need many readiness experiences in listening before he can cope with formal reading.

Similarly a child at a very limited stage of visual discrimination ability may be unable to match puzzle parts or to identify similarities and differences in pictures or designs, yet another child of the same age may be able to identify letters and digits by name and perhaps be able to write all the letters of the alphabet. Obviously one child has reached a level where he can cope with visual tasks of reading and the other needs considerable time and preparation to develop visual acuity.

What We Do with What We Discover

As can be seen on the assessment chart, Albert demonstrated very limited listening comprehension and attention span, fairly limited auditory discrimination, and somewhat limited speech fluency and oral vocabulary, yet he demonstrates adequate visual discrimination and is advanced in motor coordination. This would appear to indicate that Albert

ASSESSMENT OF READING-RELATED ABILITIES

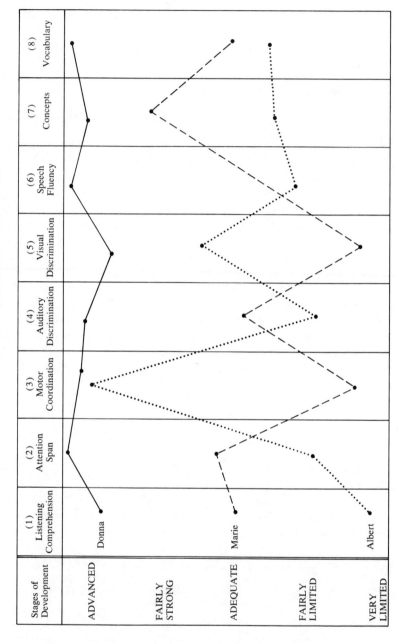

is functioning more adequately through visual modalities. This may be the place to begin in order to give him a successful start in the prereading program. Needs appear to be clearly indicated in the area of auditory skills, oral language, and attention span. All are interrelated.

Marie shows adequate development in listening comprehension and auditory discrimination but is functioning at a very limited stage of development in visual discrimination and motor abilities. Although somewhat limited in speech fluency, she demonstrates a fairly strong grasp of language concepts. Instruction needs to be geared accordingly.

Donna shows advanced development in all areas tested. To persist in a readiness program for her, based on the needs of either Marie or Albert, may be sheer waste of time and could lead to boredom and disenchantment. Failure to provide a program to challenge this child is as unreasonable as to insist that Marie should immediately be thrust into a preprimer where she must deal with printed words. Tentatively at least, we could predict that Donna is ready to read.

What We Use as Performance Criteria

We look at *what the child does* as a means of assessing ability. Far too often readiness testing is limited to results of a standardized reading readiness group test. While such tests have value as a comparative look at students within a given group, they are often very inadequate for language-different children. At best, few tests are culture-free and none can adequately evaluate the child's individual speech patterns. Therefore, we need to set up a program of evaluation that provides both formal and informal assessments.

A. Informal Observation
1. Observe the child during free play periods with other children and during teacher-directed activities. Record observations regarding language fluency, vocabulary and ability to cope with a group situation.
2. Engage the child in discussion as he plays with toys or manipulates equipment. Note attention span, ability to stay with a task, and frustration tolerance.
3. Observe the child's ability to match puzzle parts, balance blocks, manipulate movable parts of toys. Note eye-hand coordination, and part-to-whole relationships.
4. Plan individual "talk time" with each child to assess possible pronunciation problems and speech difficulties. Record dialect difference and sound problems. (See Chapter 4)

B. Formal Assessment
1. When formal tests are given to second language learners, all directives or explanations may need to be given in the first language preference as well as in English. If teachers are unable to do this, bilingual aides or parent volunteers can assist.

   The following tests and evaluation techniques are suggested as being appropriate for second language learners or children with particular language problems and/or perceptual problems.

Language Assessment

Peabody Picture Vocabulary Test[2]
A kit of pictures to test the understanding of spoken words.

Boston University Speech Sound Discrimination Picture Test[3]
Pictures to assess sound problems.

Monroe Oral Language Assessment[4]
This informal evaluation is intended to indicate levels of oral language. It is based on the following classification of a child's oral language skills:

1. How a child thinks, as revealed by the quality of his ideas.
2. How a child thinks, as revealed by the nature of his definitions of words.
3. How a child uses words, as revealed by his ability to verbalize ideas.
4. How a child uses words, as revealed by his command of sentence structure.

A rating scale is provided relative to the above four areas. Procedures are described for using this technique. (Some teachers are administering the technique in the native tongue of the child to estimate general linguistic levels).[5] It is suggested that this type of evaluation should be used along with reading-readiness test scores and the day-to-day observation of pupil behavior.

---

[2]Peabody Picture Vocabulary Test (Minneapolis: Minnesota Test Bureau).

[3]Boston University Speech Sound Discrimination Picture Test (Boston: Boston University).

[4]Marion Monroe and Bernice Rogers, *Foundations for Reading* (Chicago: Scott Foresman Company, 1964).

[5]The assessment procedures designed by Monroe were adapted and administered in Spanish to Head Start enrollees in the Tempe, Arizona Elementary Program.

Perceptual Abilities

Illinois Test of Psycholinguistic Abilities; Kirk and McCarthy[6]

Designed as a quantitative test of psycholinguistic abilities for children from ages two to nine, the test measures the following nine areas and pinpoints the areas of weakness; (1) auditory decoding; (2) visual decoding; (3) auditory-vocal association; (4) visual-motor association; (5) vocal encoding; (6) auditory-vocal automatic; (7) auditory-visual sequential; (8) visual-motor sequential; and (9) motor encoding. These tests have been specifically devised to determine which functions have developed and which are defective. For the child with language difficulties, this type of test assists the teacher in determining whether the child understands what he hears, or is able to express in words what he understands. Since it is a performance test, it is particularly useful for bilingual and bicultural students.

Purdue Perceptual Motor Survey; Kephart[7]

Designed to assess eleven visual-motor perceptual tasks, (1) identifying body parts; (2) the walking board; (3) jumping; (4) imitation of movements; (5) obstacle course; (6) angels-in-the-snow; (7) stepping stones; (8) chalkboard; (9) ocular pursuits; (10) visual achievement forms; and (11) Kraus-Weber tests. The tests are focused on visual-motor abilities, directionality, control and other tasks related to reading skills.

Visual Perception

Developmental Test of Visual Perception; Frostig[8]

Designed to test five specific visual perceptual skills, (1) eye-motor coordination; (2) figure-ground perception; (3) constancy of shape; (4) position in space; and (5) spatial relationships. The test is relatively simple to administer and specific follow-up activities are published to develop each of the five identified skills.

Mertens Visual Perception Test[9]

The Mertens Visual Perception Test was primarily designed for group and individual administration to first graders by classroom teach-

---

[6]Samuel A. Kirk and James J. McCarthy, *The Illinois Test of Psycholinguistic Abilities* (Champaign: University of Illinois Press, 1968).

[7]Newell C. Kephart and Eugene C. Roach, *The Purdue Perceptual Motor Survey* (Columbus: Charles E. Merrill Publishing, Inc., 1966).

[8]Marianne Frostig, *Developmental Test of Visual Perception* (Palo Alto, California: Consulting Psychologist Press, 1966).

[9]Marjorie K. Mertens, *Mertens Visual Perception Test* (Tempe, Arizona: Arizona State University, 1966).

ers, counselors, and those interested in diagnosing visual perceptual difficulties of children. It may also be used in diagnosing visual perceptual difficulties of youngsters in all primary grades. The scoring is simple and requires no special training. Testing time is approximately twenty minutes.

The test is comprised of six sub-tests, each representing an area of visual perception which is closely related to reading ability, (1) *design copying* (involves part-whole relationships); (2) *design reproduction* (tests visual-motor ability); (3) *framed pictures* (tests discrimination of parts); (4) *design completion* (test of closure); (5) *spatial recognition* (tests space orientation of letter-like shapes); (6) *visual memory.*

The total score may be used as an indication of overall ability in visual perceptual areas, while individual sub-test scores serve as diagnostic measures of deficit areas, and those in need of remediation before reading efficiency may be obtained.

Auditory Discrimination

Some children are slower than their peers to develop auditory discrimination. This ability is highly related to the development of speech and is both directly and indirectly related to reading. Assessing the level of auditory development is particularly important in determining which students are ready for or can profit from phonic instruction.

An auditory discrimination test of particular interest is one developed by Wepman.[10] This test is a simple method of determining a child's ability to recognize the fine differences that exist between the phonemes used in English speech. It measures only the ability to hear those distinctions. The test is simple to administer in that the child is required only to shake or nod his head, or in some way indicate whether pairs of words pronounced to him are the same or different. For example, the examiner says, "I am going to read some words to you—two words at a time. If they are exactly the same, say yes or nod your head. Say no or shake your head if they are different."

The word pairs selected were matched for familiarity by selecting words from the Lorge Thorndike Teacher's Word Book of 30,000 words (1944).

According to the author every possible match of phonemes used in English was made within phonetic categories; for example, words

---

[10]Joseph M. Wepman, *Auditory Discrimination Test* (Chicago, Illinois, 950 E. 59th Street, 1958). The test consists of a one page test form and a two page manual of directions.

having the simple stops (p, t, k) were matched only with other phonemes within that category. To illustrate, words within that category include such pairs as follows:

*t*in—*p*in (different)

pa*t*—pac*k* (different)

cor*k*—por*k* (same)

sha*k*e—sha*p*e (different)

cha*p*—cha*p* (same)

Vowel comparisons are presented in terms of tongue and lips position. Here too, the objective is to determine the child's ability to hear the difference between similar vowel sounds. Examples of vowel pairs are as follows:

b*u*m—b*o*mb (different)

sh*oa*l—sh*a*wl (different)

l*a*th—l*a*sh (same)

p*e*n—p*i*n (different)

k*i*ng—k*i*ng (same)

Two forms of the test are available for test-retest evaluation. Each form consists of thirty word pairs that differ in a single phoneme in each pair and ten word pairs which do not differ.

The examiner reads the word pairs aloud in a normal conversational tone, then records responses by checking in an X or Y column to indicate correct and incorrect response. A scoring chart is provided to indicate the level of auditory discrimination for a particular age group.

The test is designed for use with children between the ages of five and eight. It may also be useful for testing older children who appear to have delayed speech accuracy.

A sampling population of 489 children, comprising all ethnic groups, was used in the statistical analysis.

FOUNDATIONAL STEPS FOR READING

The beginning reader is thrust into a cluster of tasks somewhat simultaneously. Because students have varied capacities and differing levels of perceptual skills as well as linguistic abilities, the tasks differ for each child. If speech patterns in standard English are not well developed or if the student has a meager fund of language concepts, first steps have to do with the following:

1. Transferring meanings from the individual speech repertoire to in-school standard English.
2. Building a fund of language concepts in English.
3. Developing auditory acuity in detecting contrasts between the target language and the first (or native) language.
4. Associating the visual symbols of English with the sounds of English.

A reading readiness program must be aimed toward certain expected behaviors:

A growing awareness
1. of shapes, sizes, quantities and their relationships
2. of sounds and the rhythmic patterns created by sound combinations
3. of sequence and progression
4. of action and consequence

A growing sensitivity
1. to differences and likenesses in symbolic forms
2. to finer visual discrimination of words having similar rhythm patterns
3. to words in English that begin with the same sound as words in the native language (for second language learners)
4. to English sentence pattern rhythms

An expanding oral English vocabulary
1. English words to use as alternatives to Spanish, Indian, or other non-English words
2. a basic need vocabulary for immediate use

Growing fluency in oral expression
1. in using his own language if he is bilingual or monolingual in a language other than English
2. in expressing himself in English with his teacher and his peers
3. in acquiring simple basic sentence patterns

A growing ability to listen
1. for pleasure, appreciation, and information
2. for the purpose of improving articulation
3. for the purpose of responding to the teacher and to peers

An expanding fund of concepts
1. about family, school and neighborhood
2. about pets and animals
3. about work and play
4. about self and others
5. about time, space, and quantitative relationships

Guiding the Second Language Learner

1. Find the level of the child's receptive language.
2. Discover the modality through which the child learns best.
3. Plan experiences that are conducive to discovery, experimentation, and invention.
4. Maintain a climate that insures the child's feeling of security and well being.
5. Set up situations where organized play can become a vehicle for language growth and cognitive development.
6. Use real objects and concrete experiences.
7. Work individually with children at every opportunity.
8. Utilize volunteers and aides who are bilingual or who speak the native tongue of non-English-speaking students.
9. Use the child's native tongue to explain new ideas, new concepts, or new vocabulary in English.
10. Plan activities that involve multisensory experiences.
11. Demonstrate rather than verbalize.
12. Maintain continuity in learning experiences.
13. Utilize the out-of-doors as a learning environment.
14. Use playground games and activities as a means of teaching English, particularly verbs and verb phrases.
15. Evaluate language level and measure language growth during the informal free play activities.

AUDITORY FUNCTIONING AND THE READING PROCESS

Many children have to be taught a new way of hearing. Preschool auditory experiences may or may not have prepared them to hear finer distinctions in sounds or to develop auditory memory. Reading will place high priority on the ability to store and then to retrieve auditory information. The ability to attack a new word or to recall a previously learned word depends upon the student's ability to call up the auditory memory of the word or phonemic part of the word upon seeing the visual form.

Wepman's research[11] in the area of auditory perception has many applications for the reading teacher. He defines perceptual functioning as a process of (1) *discrimination,* (2) *memory,* (3) *sequential patterning,* and (4) *intermodal transfer.* The last, *intermodal transfer,* is considered by a number of researchers to be of critical importance. The term is used to describe the student's ability to shift from one modality to another. The ease and rapidity with which a child, upon seeing the signal (the word) can call up previously learned visual forms of the word and then shift to previously received auditory forms, has much to do with success in word perception.

In monolinguals, the shift from one modality to another is simply a matter of discrimination, memory and matching of written words with word meanings in the speech repertoire. In second language learners, there may not be a language meaning in the memory bank to match the second-language signal. To further complicate the problem, the child may have in his memory bank such auditory forms as, "shicken" for chicken, "sheep" for ship, "flow" for floor, or "tum" for thumb. In this case, shifting modalities of visual and auditory perception is a much more complex process.

In the Raab, Deutsch and Freedman[12] study, the investigators discovered that poor readers showed significantly greater difficulty in making cross-modal shift from one sensory modality to another than did normal readers. In a later study, Katz and Deutsch[13] also reported the same finding.

Rivers' research studies[14] are relevant to this topic. She says the amount of information a particular word conveys is a "function of the number of possible alternatives which would be meaningful to us in that position." She points out that in the native language, we use a number of cues we have built up through our experiences with language.

Second language learners are either bereft or partially bereft of these supports and cues. They must hear everything, hear it clearly, and then remember. *The native speaker patches together fragments of speech*

---

[11]Joseph M. Wepman, "Auditory Discrimination, Speech and Reading," *Elementary School Journal,* 40 (March, 1960): 325–33.

[12]S. Raab, M. Deutsch, and A. M. Freedman, "Perceptual Shifting and Set in Normal School Children of Different Reading Achievement Levels," *Perceptual Motor Skills* 10 (1960): 187–92.

[13]Phyllis Katz and Martin Deutsch, *Visual and Auditory Efficiency and its Relationship to Reading in Children* (Washington, D.C.: U.S. Office of Education Cooperative Research Project No. 1099, 1963), p. 45.

[14]Wilga M. Rivers, *The Psychologist and The Foreign Language Teacher* (Chicago: University of Chicago Press, 1964), pp. 107–108.

or reconstructs the whole message from parts of the original. Second language learners, or monolinguals in English whose speech patterns are significantly substandard English, are not prepared for the sequence of speech sounds of standard English and are therefore cut off from supports the native speaker or fluent speaker employs.[15]

Although there remains a great need for research to determine the full relationship of auditory discrimination to success in reading, a preponderance of evidence supports the belief that auditory discrimination training is vitally important in beginning instruction and that such training does contribute to proficiency in word recognition.

The Teacher's Role

The teacher's role is to provide many opportunities for the child to sharpen auditory acuity and to build up a memory bank of auditory clues. This means that there will be many opportunities for children to become verbal *participators* instead of *passive receivers*. It means that the teacher will need to spend time with small groups as well as with individuals in assessing listening ability and auditory acuity. It means, too, that there will never be ample time to work individually with individuals *unless* the teacher capitalizes on every resource possible.

Hopefully, there will be teacher aides, volunteer aides, or high school tutors who are available to the teacher to provide maximum opportunity for one-to-one relationships. Individual needs are crucial in classrooms where there are second-language learners.

PROVISIONS FOR AUDITORY PERCEPTUAL DEVELOPMENT

Areas of Concern:
Hearing and producing the sounds of English.
Becoming sensitive to the melody of English sentence patterns.
Understanding, using, and remembering what is heard.
Discriminating likenesses and differences in spoken words.
Hearing and producing words beginning and ending with the same sounds.
Identifying and producing words having similar sound patterns within words.

---

[15]Rivers, p. 108.

Expectations	Activities
Attention span should develop to the point that the student can profit from a directed speaking-listening experience.	Small groups share and tell time (Bilinguals should be encouraged to share and tell in the native language as well as in English)

Student should be able to demonstrate through verbal reaction and/or dramatization that he can understand and remember what he hears.	Teacher tells or reads a story, students re-tell, dramatize, or participate by pantomiming as the teacher reads. (For bilinguals, stories should be read and told in both languages. Teacher and teacher aide can "team" in such an activity)
	
	Use various types of puppets:
	–to portray characters in stories
	–to give verbal directions
	
	  "Simon Says"
	  "Touch the back of your head"
	
	–to model difficult sound patterns
	
	(Both teacher and student use hand puppets)
	
	TEACHER: "I'm Bozo. I have big black shoes." "What kind of shoes do you have?"
	
	STUDENT: "I'm Becky." "I have little blue shoes," etc.

Student should be able to demonstrate a growing awareness of sound patterns and be able to produce such patterns when given oral clues.	Hearing, repeating, nursery rhymes. Completion of rhymes or cadence patterns
	
	(a) rhyming elements:
	  pat hat _____
	  I saw a clown,
	  Standing up side _____.
	
	(b) rhythmic sequence:
	  skipping, tipping _____.
	
	(c) structure patterns:
	  caught a mouse, in the_____
	  chased a toad, down the _____

Expectations	Activities
Students should be able to produce tone-level responses.	Singing responses such as; teacher sings name of child, each syllable at a different tone level. "Ro ber to ." Child responds by singing, "I am here ."
The student should be able to identify words in English that have similar sound patterns within the word.	Activities and games such as, "Say another one like this," Mother (*brother*), night (*light*), clock (*sock*), man (*tan*), pin (*fin*), tells (*bells*), sing (*ring*).
Students will be expected to discriminate similarities and differences in phonemic elements at the beginning and within words.	Teacher directed activities such as: Teacher: "Listen, *bake, bun, Bob,*" "Barbara you say another word that begins the same way." Students respond by producing words beginning with phoneme *b*.
Students should be able to demonstrate their ability to hear all the consonant phonemes (including digraphs) by orally producing the same phoneme when given the oral stimulus.	Teacher: "Listen, *chop, chair, cheese.*" "You say another word that begins the same way." Student produces word beginning with phoneme *ch*. Records and tapes are available commercially for auditory discrimination experiences to add to the teacher-made tapes that may be produced.
As awareness of phonemic elements is refined, students should be able to hear (a) beginning and ending sounds in minimal pairs (b) vowel sounds within words.	Game Activity: Prepare cards to indicate; (a) same (b) different

Expectations	Activities
	As teacher repeats paired words, student holds up card indicating if words are the same or different.
	A. Consonant elements
	(1) (2) (3) (4) (5)
	pig pick pin tuck price
	big pig pin tug prize
	B. Vowel elements
	(1) (2) (3) (4) (5)
	sheep bit map bake pain
	ship beat map beg pen
	The activity is reinforced by providing pictures the child may hold up as he pronounces selected words.

PROVISIONS FOR EXTENDING SPEECH FLUENCY

In the simple day-to-day business of following directions, putting toys in place, preparing for games, putting materials away, getting ready for lunch, and the endless activities of classroom living, language growth can become a functional process. The natural repetition of directives accompanied by movement and activity provides purpose for speech development.

Strategies	Activities
Teach language in functional situations	Provide a play-house area:
	1. group students so they may learn informally from each other.
Use games, toy play, and "staged" situations to teach concepts of *size, place, quantity, time* and *quality*.	2. use directed activities for pattern practice.
	Teacher, "What is this, Rosalie?" (points to play-house articles)
1. Size relationship terms. *large and small* *big and little*	Rosalie, "This is a pan" (kettle, spoon, broom, etc.)

Strategies	Activities
2. Place relationship terms. *here and there* *near (close) and far* *up and down* *over and under* 3. Quantitative terms. *number words (one through ten)* *many, more, much* *some, all, none, few* *today, tomorrow, yesterday* *now, soon, later, after a while* *day and week* *morning, afternoon, night* *before, after, until* 4. Qualitative relationship terms. *hard, soft, rough, smooth* *sharp, dull, heavy, light* *nice, new, old, pretty,* *beautiful* *happy, sad* 5. Use concrete objects to teach the terms: *in, on, above, below,* *inside, outside, right,* *left*	Teacher, "What is this, Rosalie?" (points to an iron, ironing board, egg beater, etc., each requiring the article *an.*) Rosalie: "This is (a) (an) iron." (Teacher aids in making the transition from *a kettle, a spoon, a broom,* to *an iron, an ironing board, an egg beater,* etc.) Activity would include other transitions; *This* is a spoon; *these* are spoons; *these* are grapes; *those* are plums, etc. 3. Utilize "Toy Talk"[16] as a vehicle for language-concept development: "A large truck." "A little truck." "Put the truck over here." "Put the ladder inside the truck." "The truck is under the bridge." (Relationship terms are utilized) 4.

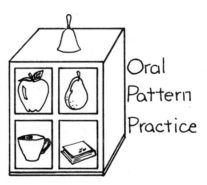

Oral Pattern Practice

---

[16]The term "Toy Talk" is taken from the experimental studies of Dr. Robert Strom and Mrs. Caryl Steere at Arizona State University. In this study parents have been involved in a laboratory situation utilizing toys as a means of developing vocabulary and oral language concepts.

Strategies	Activities
	Put the apple in the box.
	Put the apple on the box.
	Put the bell on the right side.
	Put the book on the left side, etc.

Strategies	Activities
Use out-door play as a means of building language facility;	
(a) following and giving directions;	1. Games necessitate dialogue involving specific language concepts: "Lupe is first." "Edwardo is second." "Close your eyes." "Open your eyes." "Pick up the ball." "Run to Alice," etc.
(b) extend vocabulary through directed play as students use swings, slides and other playground equipment, and as they play organized games;	2. Teacher: "Roberto is climbing up, up, up." "He is coming down, down, down." Student: "I'm climbing up." "I'm coming down." Teacher: "One, two, three, I'll throw the ball to Marie." (Students model, repeat, and invent)
(c) provide activities to coordinate body movements with rhythm patterns of language.	3. Students chant lines in synchopated rhythm with rope-jumping; "I asked my mother for fifteen cents. To watch the elephant jump the fence He jumped so high he touched the sky And didn't come back 'til the 4th of July.
Use functional situations to help students transform oral structure patterns.	1. Teacher directed activities:

Strategies	**Activities**

Using pictures or articles:

As students gain in language power more highly structured oral language patterns can be introduced using basic kernel sentences.

Teacher models and guides oral patterns:

"What's this?" "It's a spoon."
"What's this?" "It's an apple."
"What's this?" "These are scissors."
"What's this?" "This is a loaf of bread."
"What's this?" "It's some fruit."

Common sentence patterns (adapted from Roberts' types of kernel sentences)

1. DNV, My dog barks.
2. VN, Run Leslie!
3. V (adv) Come here.
4. V (prep) (D)N, Look at my picture.
5. (D) NV (adj) This lemon is sour.
6. (D) NV (adv) My sister is here.
7. N V (D) N, Mom gave me some ice cream.
8. NV (D) N, Lupe painted a picture.
9. NVbe(adv) My sister is here.
10. NVbe(adj) Roberto is hungry.
11. NVbe(D)N, Johnny is my cousin.

2. Oral language pattern practice; teacher uses games, puppets, play activties, and socio-drama to motivate pupil to produce selected patterns.

Examples:

1. DNV Pattern
Teacher (using clown puppet): "Bozo can jump," (demonstrates) "What can your puppet do?" Student (using his puppet): "Happy can dance." (demonstrates)

2. (D)NV (Adj) Pattern

Teacher (using real or artificial fruit models): "This apple is sweet and crunchy."

Student: "This banana is soft and mushy."

Strategies	Activities
	3. Converting Statements to questions
	Teacher: "Did Lupe paint this picture?"
	Student: "No, Tony painted this picture."

PROVSIONS FOR DEVELOPING TACTILE PERCEPTION

The linguistically disadvantaged child may have to depend more on his tactile and visual modality than on auditory perception in the beginning. Tactile sensation is an important part of sensory learning.

At the beginning level, children should be given much support in utilizing the tactile, kinesthetic sense. Some children appear to have greater recall when they trace letters or figures in the air, or on their own arm. Experiences involving the tactile senses appear to be an important part of the reading readiness program.

Activities: A touch and tell box

The student reaches in a box to "feel" the objects inside. Included in the concealed contents are objects or materials that are hard, soft, silky, rough, sticky, and so on. The student describes what he has touched. Whether the object is rough bark, smooth satin, or spongy rubber, he has the experience of producing words to express his sensory impressions.

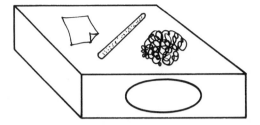

Materials such as sandpaper, velvet, or sponge may be glued to the out-side of smaller boxes. Children may choose from a random selection of articles and decide which belongs in a particular box. Such classification offers not only the experience in perceiving relationships but helps the child make finer discrimination.

Later activities. Letters having hard sounds (c as in cake, g as in gold) can be cut from sandpaper, while letters having the soft sound (c as in city, g as in giant) can be cut from flocked or velvet texture paper.

Tracing letters or words in the air may help a child "fix" the image in his mind.

Many teachers provide individual chalk boards and small erasers for students. Beginning writing experiences with chalk and chalkboard afford more freedom of movement, more tactile experience, and permit the teacher to see all the students' work at a glance.

A shoe box lid containing salt, preferably tinted with food coloring, can be used as a means of providing tactile experiences. In the readi-ness period, the student can copy figure designs by simply tracing the design in the salt with his finger. Later he can write letters or words. Of-ten this is helpful to the child who reverses letters or digits.

VISUAL PERCEPTION

One of the most specific and the most obvious of reading-related abilities in the development of prereading instruction is that of visual acuity. A child is unlikely to be ready to read symbols unless he is able to do the following:

1. Focus attention on printed material at near-point position (four-teen to eighteen inches from the eyes).

2. Differentiate between symbols having the same form but differing in position.
3. Note slight difference in form, line, and size of letter symbols and match symbols that are just alike.

Obviously such abilities entail physical factors as well as environmental experience. Children who have handled books, puzzles, pictures, and been involved with tasks requiring near-point visual acuity are usually better prepared to begin reading. If a youngster has followed along as an adult has read to him, he has already learned that print runs from left to right (in English) and then sweeps back to the beginning of the next line. Some parents spend considerable time with their children observing rocks, leaves, designs and so on, in such a way that the child has noted minute differences in shapes, designs, color, and textures.

It's a fortunate child who has been intellectually stimulated and visually motivated to be curious about his world and investigate things in his environment in his early preschool years. When he isn't, and doesn't, it's the teacher's job to provide many opportunities for matching, comparing, measuring, manipulating, touching, and exploring the world of objects and symbols.

To perceive visually is to "see with understanding." Any restrictions on visual functioning may interfere with that process, whether this relates to visual acuity, focusing, comfort, or ability to sustain attention.

Frostig's work in perceptual development has influenced many primary educators to focus more time and attention on specific visual perceptual skills. This investigator has pointed out that a child who has a lag in his perceptual development may have difficulty in recognizing objects and their relationships to each other in space and that this causes him to be clumsy and poorly coordinated. The resulting confusion and emotional stress make academic learning difficult.[17] The abilities to (1) sense spacial relationships, (2) focus on stimuli in the midst of many stimuli, (3) perceive laterally (b and d differ only in directional characteristics) and (4) coordinate eye-hand movement appear to be important factors in reading success.

Visual Functioning and the Reading Process

Russell described the reading act as a relatively simultaneous process involving the following:

---

[17] Marianne Frostig, *Developmental Test of Visual Perception* (Palo Alto, California: Consulting Psychologist Press, 1966).

. . . sensation of light rays on the retina of the eye reaching the brain, perception of separate words and phrases, functioning of eye muscles with exact controls, immediate memory for what has been read, remote memory based on the reader's experience, and the organizing of materials so that finally it can be used in some way.[18]

Small wonder that some children have difficulty in learning to read! Visual and auditory abilities, experiential background, interest, memory, attitude, drive, and a host of sub-factors are involved. The cruciality of vision, however, is quite evident. Nothing takes place if the subject cannot see clearly enough to carry out the reading act and there is little doubt that many students are poor readers simply because of sight problems that have gone undetected or untreated year after year.

Visual Deficiencies

Although no teacher is expected to be a diagnostician of visual disabilities, each teacher has the obligation to detect any physical impairment that interferes with learning. Early detection of visual problems is particularly important. Defects of muscle function which control eye movement, *strabismus* (crossed eyes caused by lack of coordination between both eyes) and *heterophoria* (a muscle imbalance preventing fusion of two images from both eyes into a single image) are often found to be causes of reading failure. *Myopia* (nearsightedness) and *hyperopia* (farsightedness), which are easily correctable, can go undetected unless alert teachers observe students closely.

Identification of visual disabilities in the very young child are often difficult. The child who has always had such a handicap has no basis for comparison. He is not aware that his vision differs from others and he is not likely to tap his teacher on the shoulder and say, "I have a problem. I can't see clearly!" Nevertheless, common sense tells us that our own experiences with visual fatigue or visual discomfort should alert us to symptomatic behavior in a child.

Kirk urges that children of preschool and school age be observed closely for the following indications of visual difficulty:

1. How the child uses his eyes: tilting his head, holding objects too close to his eyes, rubbing his eyes, squinting, displaying sensitivity to bright light, and rolling his eyes.

---

[18]David H. Russell, *Children Learn to Read* (Boston: Ginn and Company, 1961), p. 99.

2. Inattention to visual objects or visual tasks such as looking at pictures or reading.
3. Awkwardness in games requiring eye-hand coordination.
4. Avoidance of tasks that require close eye work.
5. Any complaints about inability to see.[19]

Most schools have now recognized the limitations of the Snellen Visual Screening Test. The test probably is adequate to determine whether an individual is visually capable of driving a car safely because it does measure central distance visual acuity. However, the Snellen Test does not measure near-point vision, peripheral vision, convergence ability, fusion ability, or muscular imbalance. Far-point acuity has little to do with in-the-classroom visual tasks other than in chalkboard or large chart tasks.

Many schools have expanded visual screening programs to include more suitable tests than the Snellen Charts. Kirk[20] recommends the Massachusetts Vision Test, the Keystone Telebinocular, and the Orthorater as being most suitable for school use. At best, such devices serve only to identify students with suspected visual deficiencies so that proper referral can be made to opthalmologists, optometrists, or other specialists.

Near-point and Far-point Vision

In preschool years, most children use parallel vision the greater part of the day. The eyes are not required to fuse images as in near-point visual tasks. In far-point vision, two separate images are reflected on the retina requiring little muscle control. Unless children have handled books, worked with puzzles or other activities requiring near-point visual functioning, they are often unready for reading from books. One might speculate about the influence of preschool play activity on visual acuity and then pose a question. Is it possible that girls are more conditioned to reading tasks by their preschool experiences than boys?

A number of studies are reported by Heilman[21] concerning sex differences in learning to read. The preponderance of evidence cited in numerous studies reported suggests that girls, as a group, measure

---

[19]Samuel A. Kirk, *Educating Exceptional Children* (Boston: Houghton Mifflin Company, 1962), pp. 200–203.

[20]Kirk, p. 202.

[21]Arthur Heilman, *Principles and Practices of Teaching Reading,* 3rd ed. (Columbus, Ohio: Charles E. Merrill Publishing Co., 1972), pp. 32–36.

higher in reading achievement in the early grades than boys and that girls tend to score higher than boys on certain reading readiness tests.

It is very possible that girls are involved more with toys, games, and picture book activities that develop visual perceptual abilities in the preschool years. Many parents perceive the boys' role as being quite different from the girls' role. It may be that parents are prone to condition boys for the "male role" by encouraging out-of-door play and by providing vehicular toys, balls, ball bats, blocks, and similar large muscle toys, while girls are usually given books, toy dishes, beadwork, weaving sets, and similar materials that involve near-point work. While this may merely indicate that such a difference between the two types of activities relates more to attention span and concentration than to actual visual perceptual skills, it might have something to do with sex difference in beginning reading regardless. Certainly reading does require close attention and a great deal of concentration for young children whose growing bodies require movement and physical action. Research is much needed in this area since it might have many implications for the reading readiness program relative to visual training for boys.

Eye Movement

Reading printed material requires a number of specific eye movement skills, abilities that are learned behaviors. With the aid of eye movement cameras, researchers have been able to record on film the patterns of eye movement. Through these recorded film studies, a number of discoveries have been made. Russell describes some of these findings as follows:

1. Actual visual perception takes place only when the eyes fixate (focus) at certain points in a line of print. Good adult readers make three to five fixations per line while poor child readers make nine to fifteen. The average length of time for fixation is one-eighth to one-quarter second.

2. Regression refers to the backward movement of the eyes on a line of print. Good adult readers make one regression in every three or four lines, while poor child readers make three or more per line.

3. The good reader has a reading span (distance between two fixations) of thirteen to fourteen spaces while poor readers have an average of six spaces.[22]

[22]Russell, pp. 99–106.

Eye movement varies according to the purpose of reading. Factual material with details requires slower, more painstaking reading. Thus, we would expect more fixations per line in information type reading even in the efficient reader. Poor readers, however, usually do not exhibit the ability to "shift gears" for different types of reading. Commonly, the poor reader makes many fixations per line in all his reading.

Eye Movement Training

The primary teacher plays an important role in setting the stage for good eye movement. It is very possible that the "Round-Robin" oral reading in a classroom where students are required to *keep the place*, has contributed to regressive eye movement. Silent reading is more rapid than oral reading. If the silent reader is required to follow along while someone reads orally, he will find himself making regressions regardless of the proficiency of the oral reader. What happens if the oral reading performance is poor is very obvious. Students should not be required to read copy while someone reads aloud. Silent reading and oral reading serve two different purposes in the first place. Secondly, eye movement may be affected adversely when students are required to pace silent reading rate with oral reading rate.

Initial experiences in reading should be designed in such a way that the student perceives units of thoughts instead of isolated words. During the readiness period, nursery rhymes and familiar songs may be written in manuscript on the chalkboard or on a chart. As children sing or recite the material from memory (even though they may not yet know the words) the teacher sweeps her hand beneath the thought units in the rhythmic movement of natural speech, from left to right across the line and then diagonally back to the line below. Directionality is a learned skill and eye movement habits are formed early.

VISUAL DISCRIMINATION SKILLS

Among questions researchers have sought to answer are the following:

1. What effect does training in recognition of nonverbal forms (geometric figures and designs) have on progress in learning to read?
2. Are there different types of "perceivers" among young children?
3. What specific types of visual perceptual skills are most closely related to reading?

4. Does the knowledge of the names of letters or knowledge of the sequence of the alphabet predict reading success?

Relationships to Reading

Goins' very significant work in visual discrimination revealed a number of findings very important to reading teachers. It was the purpose of her study to: (1) ascertain the relationship between reading ability and visual perception, and (2) determine the effects of visual training on progress in learning to read. Her conclusions were that "different pupils clearly use two distinct methods of attacking the same perceptual tasks."[23] Findings relate closely to Wepman's research indicating that some children are visual learners and some are auditory learners. Both researchers conclude that beginning teaching methods should make use of both sight and sound techniques and that teachers should make every attempt to determine by which modality the child learns best.

A second finding of Goins was a high correlation between certain perceptual tasks, as determined by the following:

1. A test of closure (completing a drawing with missing parts).
2. A test of reversals (finding reversed pictures in sets where others were identical).
3. Pattern copying (reproducing drawings).[24]

These three skills, *closure, reversals,* and *pattern copying* revealed high correlation with reading achievement and led Goins to two conclusions, (1) that there is a need for revision of current reading readiness tests, and (2) that tests measuring *strength of closure* should be included in readiness testing. Closure refers to the ability to perceive and keep in mind a perceptual whole. Efficient reading, Goins concluded, involves the ability to hold in mind the wholeness of the word phrase or sentence while simultaneously attending to individual words or parts of words.

Letter Recognition and Letter Names

Considerable research relates to the question concerning letter names. Bond and Dykstra's[25] first grade studies indicated that knowledge of letter names is the best predictor of beginning reading success.

[23]Jean Turner Goins, *Visual Perceptual Abilities and Early Reading Progress,* Supplementary Educational Monographs No. 78 (Chicago: University of Chicago Press, 1958), p. 50.

[24]Goins, pp. 78–81.

[25]Guy L. Bond and Robert Dykstra, *U.S. Department of Health, Education and Welfare Project No. X001 Final Report* (Minneapolis: University of Minnesota, 1967).

Durrell's[26] research indicated that familiarity with letter forms was essential to perception needed to discriminate between words and concluded from his series of studies at Boston University that most reading difficulties could be prevented by instruction in letter names and sounds followed by phonic instruction. Barrett[27] concluded that the ability to discern likenesses and differences among words is of greater significance than the ability to discriminate between letter forms.

An interesting point to raise, however, is whether or not children who knew letter names were tested to see if they also knew sounds. If so, the research might only be verifying the finding of Hester,[28] Robinson,[29] Hildreth,[30] and many others who have concluded from studies that auditory clues, knowledge of letter sounds, and the ability to blend or fuse phonemes in words are the skills most closely linked with reading success.

Relationships to Writing

While evidence appears to be inconclusive regarding the importance of letter recogniton and knowledge of letter names as a prerequisite to reading, there is no question about the importance of these abilities in writing. If children are to begin writing early they must be able to produce all letters in both capital and lower case forms. For practical purposes, if for no other reason, children need names for the symbols they write. Therefore, there appears to be justification for teaching students to *recognize, name,* and *write* all letters of the alphabet early in the primary program. The process begins of course with training in visual discrimination.

---

[26]Donald D. Durrell and Helen Murphy, "Reading Readiness," *Journal of Education,* December, 1963, p. 5.

[27]Thomas C. Barrett, "The Relationships Between Measures of Pre-Reading Visual Discrimination and First Grade Reading Achievement: A Review of Literature," *Reading Research Quarterly* 1 (Fall, 1965): 51–76.

[28]Kathleen B. Hester, "A Study of Phonetic Difficulties in Reading," *Elementary School Journal* 43 (November, 1942): 171–73.

[29]Helen M. Robinson, "Factors Which Affect Success in Reading," *Elementary School Journal* 55 (January, 1955): 263–69.

[30]Gertrude H. Hildreth, "The Role of Pronouncing and Sounding in Learning to Read," *Elementary School Journal* 55 (November, 1954) 141–47.

PROVISIONS FOR VISUAL PERCEPTION

Gross Discrimination

Expectations	*Activities*
Students should be able to attend to near-point visual tasks for periods long enough to complete reasonable task assignments.	Provide a library center where books may be handled, pictures may be "read," children may listen and "follow along" to taped stories. Provide games, puzzles, and manipulative toys that require matching of shapes, designs, colors, and parts of pictures. Pictures may be pasted on cardboard backing and cut into vertical, horizontal, and/or diagonal strips. Children match parts in "rebuilding the picture."
Students should be able to demonstrate ability to coordinate eye-hand movement.	Have students cut and paste pictures from magazines and mail order catalogues on sheets labeled with such captions as: I can see things to eat, I can see things to wear, I can see things that keep me warm, etc. Let child weave colored yarn into loosely woven fabric or webbed material.
Student should be able to demonstrate: a. ability to discriminate part-whole relationships,	Ask student to fill in the missing part of the pictures;

Expectations	*Activities*
b. ability to complete (close) a design,	Finish the picture

c. ability to recall a visual sequence,	String your beads like this:

d. ability to sort and classify pictures and/or objects into categories and classes.	Ask child to group pictures into classifications, i.e. farm animals, foods, fruit, etc.
	Cut ads from magazines; some duplicates, some similar except for one item. Have children choose the ones that are alike and the ones that have differences and tell why.

DISCRIMINATION AND IDENTIFICATION OF LETTER SYMBOLS

We can expect that discrimination of letter forms will require rather specific skill training. It seems logical to begin training directly on letter forms rather than to assume that training in unrelated geometric forms will transfer. Such training entails the following:

1. Associating letter shapes and letter symbols
2. Matching letter forms from memory
3. Closure of partial letter forms
4. Tactile tracing from memory
5. Identifying a specific letter in a sequence of letters
6. Matching word forms to word configuration patterns

Strategies

The twenty-six lower case manuscript letters conform to twelve general shape patterns and the twenty-six capital letters conform to nine shape patterns. Shown in the figures below are both sets of patterns. Below each pattern are letter symbols that "fit" into the pattern.

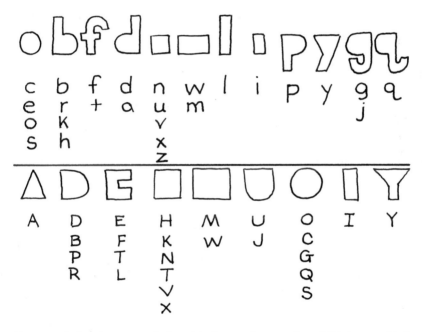

By associating letter symbols with letter shapes, the child is provided with a visual memory clue. The strategy for utilizing letter shape patterns is described in the following.

Expectations	*Activities*
Students should be able to:	Activities to develop laterality (position in space)
a. Discriminate similarities in letter-like shapes	Step 1. Have students match patterns (templates) to pattern model.

b. Differentiate letters that have the same form but differ in position (b-d)	Step 2. Have students fit letters into shapes to develop discrimination of letter shape and *above the line, below the line perception.*

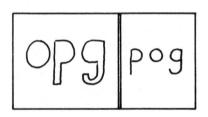

	(Continue with all letters and patterns)
c. Discriminate part-whole relationship of letter forms	Step 3. Have students trace and complete letter forms to develop visual memory and learn letter name.

Expectations	*Activities*
d. Complete letter forms by closure	Examples of "O" pattern
e. Identify letters by name	

f. Independently write each letter when given the letter name	(*The "cue" letters are cut from a rough textured paper to provide tactile stimulus)
	The activity is repeated for each pattern set.
g. Identify lower case letters with capital letters	Step 4. Prepare packs of cards, one pack for capital letters, another pack for lower case letters. Children can work in pairs to match sets.
h. Utilize word form configuration clues	Step 5. Provide activities to sensitize students to word pattern configuration clues in such activities as:

Example:

Teacher: "Do you want to go hunting?"

Listen:
"Hundreds of words,
Thousands of words
Sly as little foxes.
Follow them now,
I'll show you how
To put them in little boxes!"

Teacher: "Look at the words in the boxes. Find another box just like the first one. Write "Fox" in the empty box.

EXTENDED READINGS

Asbell, Bernard. "Helping Children Grow Up Smart." *Redbook Magazine,* July, 1970, pp. 34–40.

Barrett, Thomas C. "The Relationship Between Measures of Pre-Reading Visual Discrimination and First Grade Reading Achievement: A Review of the Literature." *Reading Research Quarterly* 1 (Fall 1965):51–76.

Bernetta, Sister M. "Visual Readiness and Developmental Visual Perception for Reading." *Journal of Developmental Reading* 5 (Winter 1962): 82–86.

Deutsch, M. "The Disadvantaged Child and the Learning Process," in *Education in Depressed Areas,* ed. A. H. Passow. New York: Teacher's College Columbia University, 1963.

Duggins, Lydia A. "Auditory Perception in the Beginning Reading Program." *Southeastern Louisiana College Bulletin,* 13, January, 1956.

Goins, Jean T. *Visual Perceptual Abilities and Early Reading Progress.* Supplementary Education Monograph No. 87, Chicago: University of Chicago Press, 1958.

Jones, W. R. "A Critical Study of Bilingualism and Non-verbal Intelligence." *British Journal of Educational Psychology* 30 (1960): 71–77.

Kephart, Newell C. *The Slow Learner in the Classroom.* Columbus, Ohio: Charles E. Merrill Publishing Co., 1960.

Kirk, S. A. and J. J. McCarthy. "The Illinois Test of Psycholinguistic Abilities—An Approach to Differential Diagnosis." *American Journal of Mental Deficiencies* 66 (1961): 339–412.

Silvaroli, N. J., and W. H. Wheelock. "An Investigation of Auditory Discrimination Training for Beginning Readers." *The Reading Teacher* 20 (December 1966):247–51.

Smith, Frank. *Understanding Reading.* New York: Holt, Rinehart, and Winston, Inc., 1971. Three chapters of particular relevance are: Chapter 7—"What the Eye Tells the Brain"; Chapter 8—"What the Brain Tells the Eye"; and Chapter 9—"Letter Identification."

Smith, Henry J., and Emerald V. Dechant. *Psychology of Teaching Reading.* Englewood Cliffs, N.J.: Prentice Hall, Inc., 1961, pp. 154–155.

Spache, George D., and Evelyn B. Spache. *Reading in the Elementary School.* Boston: Allyn and Bacon, Inc., 1969. Chapter 1 and Chapter 7.

Rice, Arthur H. "Rhythmic Training and Body Balancing Prepare Child for Formal Learning." *Nation's Schools* 69 (February 1962):2–11.

Vernon, M. D. "The Psychology of Perception." *Reading Teacher* 13 (October 1959):28.

Wepman, Joseph M. "Auditory Discrimination Speech and Reading." *Elementary School Journal* 60 (1960):325–333.

_____. "The Interrelationships of Hearing, Speech, and Reading." *Reading Teacher* 14 (March 1961):245–47.

CHAPTER 6

A Beginning Reading Program for the Language-Different, Culture-Different Child

It would be difficult to determine at what point the reading readiness program phases into formalized instruction. In a broad sense, all learning is preparation for a next step. For lack of a better term, reading-readiness designates a phase of the program focused on language development, perceptual discrimination, social learnings, and motor-skill development. Particularly for the language-different students, these are concerns that must be reflected in objectives throughout the primary program.

From a developmental point of view, the reading-readiness program simply spirals into a more formalized level of instruction as the child gains maturity and skill. This building-on and building-up process is based on the notion that each child should move along a corridor bumping his head on the ceiling of his own potential.

A BALANCED APPROACH TO INSTRUCTION

In a well planned reading program there must be concern for balance in all phases of reading development. While there is no question about the importance of skill training in word recognition, comprehension ability, and study skills, these abilities serve little purpose if not used to solve problems, to secure information, to satisfy interests, and to contribute to personal growth and pleasure. Those purposes are best served when skill application is synchronized with skill training.

Three Areas of Concern

To achieve balance in instruction, there must be focus on three areas: (1) problem-centered reading, (2) personal-recreational reading, and (3) literary reading. Each is as important and as critical at primary level as at later elementary levels. If time and effort are focused solely on basic skill instruction to the neglect of implementation, the language-different student is penalized.

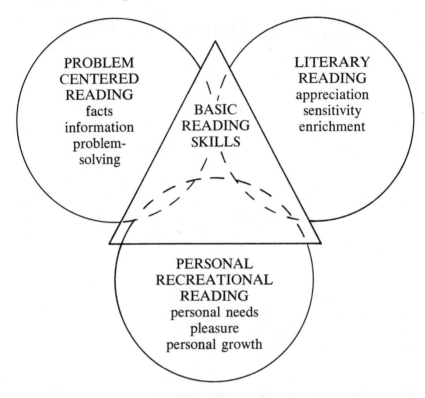

There are no definitive lines of demarcation among these three areas of instruction. Such purposes are interlocked and interdependent. The only objective of basic skill instruction is to facilitate individual ability to pursue the three general purposes of reading. The process is a "to-and-from" flow of skills, application, and enrichment of experience in reading.

However sincere the intent, the primary teacher who spends the major portion of "prime time," the morning hours of the school day, drilling children in skill exercises, leaving the last limp hour of the afternoon for science, social living studies, music, art and the "weekly reader," may be missing the point of reading instruction altogether. No one becomes a powerful swimmer by paddling in the shallow end of the pool, however expert the instruction. Expertise comes from plunging into "deeper waters" where there is need, purpose, and a full measure of self-satisfaction.

Methods and Materials Must be Matched to Purpose

Balance is achieved through use of a wide range of resources in methods, materials, and techniques. To date, no single method or material has been found to be a panacea to all problems. For language-different students particularly, it is dangerous to "fall in love" with a particular method or pledge undying faith to a particular series of published reading materials. Judicious use of materials and techniques relevant to each area of reading suggests that the teacher should know what to use and when to use it to achieve best results. If students are to cope with differentiated tasks in reading, there must be differentiated instruction.

Basal reading series offer organized, sequential, skill instruction on a systematic basis. Few teachers have the time to organize and prepare the full gamut of reading instruction experiences. Many feel unprepared to accept full responsibility for determining the sequencing of skill instruction.

Trade books keyed to the various areas of content and to the personal interests of boys and girls make library reading an integral part of the program rather than an incidental activity.

Language experience writing, teacher-composed content, experience charts and creative writing bring problem-centered reading and personal reading together through relevant and individualized application.

OBJECTIVES MUST BE ELASTIC

When language and culture differences are added to the range of individual difference among all primary children, objectives must be designed to serve as guidelines toward expected behaviors rather than hard and fast grade line goals. For some children, reading objectives must be stretched far beyond goal targets. For others, there must be adjustment to allow for slower pacing. It is totally unrealistic to suggest that any set of objectives are equally appropriate for all children at a given time. Nevertheless, if objectives are "elastic," they serve to give direction and continuity to the reading program.

In a beginning reading program, guidelines for instruction must reflect concern for (1) more specific verbal facility, (2) more specialized vocabulary power, and (3) more highly refined reading-thinking ability. Although no two students will progress at the same rate or perform at the same level, the following behaviors represent desired outcomes for the primary program:

Speaking Facility

In oral language the student should demonstrate the ability to:

1. Express himself in complete sentences rather than one word responses or nonverbal gestures.
2. Function comfortably (in English) in group talk with peers.
3. Re-tell stories or report happenings in sequential order.
4. Verbalize a definition.
5. Express an idea clearly enough to be understood.

Linguistic Ability

The student should be able to demonstrate the ability to:

1. Transform a statement to a question:
    Eddie can go with me.   Can Eddie go with me?
2. Change a positive statement to a negative:
    I can skate.   I can't skate.
3. Make noun and pronoun substitutions in a sentence:
    (Noun S)   A *bird* likes bugs.   A *turtle* likes bugs.
    (Pronoun S)   *Lupe* likes to jump rope with *Norman*.
    She likes to jump rope with *him*.
4. To expand the noun phrase:
    Our parakeet chirps.
    Our little blue parakeet chirps.
5. To expand the verb phrase:
    Our parakeet *chirps*.
    Our parakeet *chirps and eats sunflower seeds*.

Vocabulary Power

1. The student should have mastered a stock of high frequency sight words which will serve as building blocks for other words having similar sound and structure patterns.

2. He should be able to:

a. decode all of the consonant letters (graphemes) into speech sounds (phonemes) and blend combinations of those phonetic elements into meaningful words.

b. use position clues to aid in decoding the long, short, and *r*-controlled vowel symbols in such words as *bite, bit,* and *bird.*

c. decode common vowel-symbol combinations in such words as: *way, tail, out, cow, boil, toy.*

d. recognize a word in its derived form and change words into such derivatives as: *walks, walking, walked; cold, colder, coldest; boy—boys, dress—dresses, lady—ladies.*

e. use sentence context as one of the major means of word recognition and word meaning.

f. utilize an ever increasing number of high frequency spelling patterns in such words as: *hen, pen, then; pan, land, plan.*

Reading-Thinking Abilities

The student should be able to:

1. restate, in his own words, what he has read.

2. demonstrate his ability to grasp "chunks of meaning" by locating meaning units within sentences.

3. rearrange a group of pictures or series of sentences in the sequential order.

4. anticipate meaning by predicting what will happen next in a story.

5. infer meanings implied but not literally stated.

6. convey verbally or in picture form mental images he has formed from his reading.

7. demonstrate his reading-thinking abilities by making predictions of what might happen next in a story, by making judgments about events or situations, and by drawing conclusions.

8. apply what he reads to real life situations.

READING BEGINS THROUGH BROAD AVENUES OF COMMUNICATION

The reading act is so intricately enmeshed in the entire process of language, culture, and social experience that it is very difficult to determine the manner in which a child first perceives written symbols as meanings. Whether the magic moment occurs when Alberto sees his own name in print and says, "That's me!" or whether this is a gradual process through which he comes to perceive printed forms as talk written down, we cannot be sure. At any rate, we can be certain that the process is much less complicated when the written speech closely approximates the speech used by the child's parents, peers, and associates. Clearly, the child who habitually uses nonstandard forms of English, or who is speaking English as his second language, will have a difficult task, unless he is guided carefully through his first encounters with formalized reading.

Linking Reading to Writing

In the past ten years a great many reading programs have been published that reflect the influence of linguistic studies. Some focus on phonology, glorifying the coding of grapheme-phoneme correspondence. Some have used the sounds of spoken language as the framework for series of reading texts. Still others have incorporated linguistic activities as a part of techniques of word study and sentence structures. There is, however, a reading method that probably comes closer to representing a "pure" linguistic approach than any of the published reading programs. It is the process of linking the child's speech repertoire to reading. The child's speech patterns, in whatever linguistic system, are transferred to printed symbols through dictation and later used as a linguistic bridge as the student does his own writing. It is the writer's contention that this method, commonly called the language experience approach, comes closer to implementing scientific linguistic principles than many of the other so-called linguistic reading programs.

The child dictates from his own real-life experiences those things that are interesting to him. The teacher writes, from dictation, the natural forms of the child's speech. The process proceeds from spoken form to written form. The sound-to-symbol coding occurs as the child watches the teacher write the symbols that he produces vocally. The content of the material represents the concepts that are a part of the child's cultural environment. This approach implements some of the linguistic principles held to be important in second language learning:

1. Items should be presented in spoken form before they are presented in written form.
2. Content should simulate real-life situations and relate as closely as possible to the socio-cultural background of the student.
3. Language is something you understand and say before it is something you read and write.

Through the structural forms of functional language, the child encodes his own speech into written form. Through the process of transforming thoughts into words, seeing the words in printed form, and then reading them, he automatically uses the melody and structure of his own speech patterns as both meaning and word recognition clues.

ADVANTAGES AND LIMITATIONS OF THE LANGUAGE EXPERIENCE APPROACH

An Ego-involved Process

The language experience approach to reading, promoted by Lamoreaux and Lee[1] several years ago and revised, extended and adapted by many educators since that time, has been used successfully by many teachers as a means of launching students into formal reading. The key advantage of the strategy is that it is an ego-involved process. The rationale behind the approach revolves around the personal pronouns *I* and *Me*:

What *I* can think about, *I* can say.
What *I* can say, *I* can write.
What *I* can write, *I* can read.
I can read what *I* can write
and what others have written for *me* to read.[2]

It is a highly personal, individualized approach that can serve as a bridge between the child's out-of-school experience and his in-school learning experiences *if it is modified to meet particular situations* and *extended to include other strategies.*

Proceeds from Speech to Symbol

Too many times the second language learner is thrust into a process requiring him to decode a symbol representing a speech sound that simply does not exist in his speech repertoire. Most phonological systems are based on the assumption that the child can match English symbols to know speech sounds. This false assumption accounts for the failure of many phonic programs to produce any significant results among bilingual students.

---

[1]Lillian A. Lamoreaux and Doris M. Lee, *Learning to Read Through Experience* (New York: Appleton-Century-Crofts, 1943).

[2]Van Allen Roach and Claryce Allen, *An Introduction to a Language Experience Program, Level 1* (Chicago: Encyclopedia Britannica Press, 1966), pp. 1–8.

To further complicate the problem, bilingual students often are diagnosed as being weak in word recognition skills, and are given remedial phonic instruction year after year. Lack of success breeds disenchantment and an endless cycle of failure, and frustration, results. These findings can be verified in reading clinics throughout the country. The question is, "Should the encoding process precede the decoding skills?"

The thesis of this chapter is that students should have much experience in encoding sounds into letter symbols before they are placed in highly structured phonic programs. The language experience approach provides this opportunity.

Limitations

The limitation for the language-handicapped student is obvious. He cannot always "say what he can think about" in standard English. The need for oral language development cannot be bypassed and the high potential for this approach is lost unless it is combined with a strong program of oral English development. Anyone who has studied a foreign language understands the frustration of attempting to express an idea in the second language while groping for words and appropriate sentence structures.

The second limitation often cited relates to contrasts between "child talk" and printed English forms (see p. 29). Inevitably, questions are raised concerning the validity of forms of language used by children when considering the language experience approach as a strategy for reading instruction:

1. Should nonstandard dialect forms be accepted in children's writing?
2. Should the grammar of black children be incorporated in reading and writing materials used in the classroom?
3. When children dictate should the teacher use spellings that match the child's pronunciation?
4. Should experience writing from language-different students be "edited" by the teacher and written in standard English patterns?

The problem of correct usage in written and spoken forms of children's speech has always been a sensitive area. Teachers are constantly faced with the choice of accepting what the child says or writes regardless of its "correctness" or arbitrarily insisting on changing forms to conform to so-called standard English and standard English spellings.

If we accept Smith's[3] thesis that children's language is a completely valid form of language with an "adequate and systematic grammar" we would have to say that the child's speech and grammar structures, however varied because of different dialect systems, should be used.

Shuy, a sociolinguist involved in studying beginning reading materials for black children, suggests four alternative strategies for teaching reading to students with divergent dialects:

1. First teach them standard English.
2. Accept their dialect reading of traditional material written in standard English (Goodman, 1965).
3. Develop materials in standard English which minimize dialect and culture difference (Venezky, 1970).
4. Develop materials which incorporate the grammar of black children (Stewart, 1969).[4]

It is the fourth option that pertains closely to the point in question since the use of the child's language experiences forces a decision concerning usage.

Gladney[5] incorporated Shuy's fourth alternative in an experimental program to test the effectiveness of incorporating the grammar of black children in a series of reading materials for primary children. Syntactical patterns representing such forms as, *When I be running, my teacher say, Stop that,* was printed under the label of "Everyday Talk." Under the label of "School Talk" was the standard form, *When I run, my teacher says, Stop that.* The focus was placed on verb form usage and the syntactical patterns of black dialect were used in printed booklets for children to read. However, only standard orthography was used.

Although only a limited number of children were involved in the study, the results were considered to be positive by the researcher and the materials were put to use in fifty classrooms in Chicago.

The question of usage is far from being resolved. Although there appears to be general agreement among teachers that primary children

---

[3]Frank Smith, "The Learner and His Language," in *Language and Learning to Read,* ed. Richard E. Hodges and E. Hugh Rudolph (Boston: Houghton Mifflin Co., 1972), pp. 35–43.

[4]Roger W. Shuy, "Speech Differences and Teaching Strategies: How Different is Enough?" in *Language and Learning to Read,* ed. Richard E. Hodges and E. Hugh Rudolph (Boston: Houghton Mifflin Co., 1972), p. 56.

[5]Mildred R. Gladney, "A Teaching Strategy," in *Language and Learning to Read,* ed. Richard E. Hodges and E. Hugh Rudolph (Boston: Houghton Mifflin Co., 1972), pp. 73–83.

should be urged to express themselves freely in oral language without interruption or correction, there is general reluctance among many to see grammatical errors and spelling errors in print.

Thompson[6], reviewing the literature on nonstandard spellings, found no authority suggesting that misspellings be used. She believes the teacher must not use spelling that "fits the child's pronunciation" since this can lead only to confusion in learning sight words and using work attack skills. However, she urges that teachers refrain from placing value judgments on the content of experience stories or on the child's non-standard English.

Options and Alternatives

Reteaching to correct a skill is usually more difficult than teaching the correct skill in the first place. We've come to know how difficult it is to change oral language habits. If unconventional (grossly unacceptable) forms of speech and misspelled words are reinforced through writing, we may be increasing the burden for the child farther along the way. As much as possible, the child should be provided with correct forms and spellings as he needs them.

The challenge of this persistent problem appears to be in teaching the student to make use of standard forms without depreciating his cultural or social background. Most of us who seek to learn a second language would not settle for second rate instruction that results in poor usage. The question is not the goal but the process. The goal is to insure that the individual is able to function and compete favorably on two levels; individual speech acts related to social usage (*parole*) and the social part of speech which the individual must learn in conventional form (*langue*). Hopefully, such goals can be achieved through a humanistic approach as children are presented with alternatives and options. The following example may illustrate the point:

As a group of children dictated a letter to Tony who was in the hospital the teacher heard:

> Dear Tony,
> Doa'n be seek.
> Be comin' back!
> We sorry you bin gone.

---

[6]Ruby Thompson, "The Culturally Different Child," in Arthur W. Heilman's *Principles and Practices of Teaching Reading* (Columbus, Ohio: Charles E. Merrill Publishing Co., 1972), p. 57.

If we accept the idea that the teacher has the obligation to value the child's expressed idea but the responsibility to present the alternative and offer the option of more conventional terms, the process might be as follows:

"Yes, we don't want Tony to be sick."

"We can say, we don't want you to be sick," and so on.

As options are offered, speech patterns are expanded without deprecating the child's language. The teacher guards the child's meaning but introduces new forms through alternatives. The process hopefully would result in modified forms and in conventional spelling:

Dear Tony,

We don't want you to be sick.

Come back.

We are sorry you've been gone.

LINKING PERSONAL EXPERIENCE TO READING

The rather complicated business of daily living in the classroom offers the first logical need for written communication and provides a means of linking personal experience to reading.

Students' Names

When children walk into the classroom on the first day to find their name on a card designating a desk or table as *their place,* they have begun to read. Antone Bergetilli is well on his way toward letter recognition if he recognizes and can write his own name. He has sixteen letters in his name and that is over half the alphabet!

Nothing is any more personal than a name and this can and should be a very important clue for teachers. Pride in seeing one's name in print is reason enough to justify classroom name charts, but it serves as well as a reference for letter-sound relationships.

Signs, Symbols and Service Words

Classroom business and management calls for a number of signs, labels, directives and service words. Sight words accumulate rapidly as students become familiar with these functional symbols:

Labels: Book Shelf, Toy Box, Playhouse
Directives: Paint here, Find a book, Read a story
Task charts:

Clean erasers .... Billy

Feed fish .... Frank

Water plants .... Ramona

Service Words:

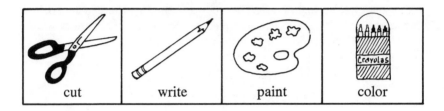

| cut | write | paint | color |

Happenings

Greetings on the chalkboard each morning may serve as the daily bulletin but incidentally introduce and use over and over again those difficult to remember service words.

Good morning.

This is Tuesday.

We are going to see a movie at 9:30.

We have a new boy in class today.

His name is Steven.

FROM SPEECH TO SYMBOL THROUGH DICTATION

Individualized reading experiences can be initiated as the teacher records what the child says. This personalized experience introduces "talk written down." As the child observes the teacher writing from his dictation, his eyes move from left to right, he sees words as wholes, and he is given auditory support as the teacher repeats as she writes.

Picture Talk

The painting easel is as important to reading as to artistic expression. Children's pictures symbolize meanings. It is the first step in transferring thought to symbolic representation. From a first grade child came one simple picture and a "chunk of meaning" but a giant step toward reading in his second language.

Realism is reflected as first grade children dictate from observation.

The girl that got arrested and the policeman were walking across the street. They were going to jail.

The structure and the vocabulary represent natural language and serve as an index to mental age and social maturity. Robin's story simply reflects the facts of life.

Randy interpreted the situation as he saw it:

The policeman got two people and put them in jail. Then he turned off the light and they couldn't see.

This story was dictated to the teacher following a field trip to the zoo. It was typed and placed in a booklet along with a story from every other class member. "Our Zoo Book" became a reading book for the class.

I liked everything.
The lions weren't in the same place that they were last year.
The zebras were in the lions cage, this time.

The baby lions were so tiny and cute.
There were four of them.
They are cubs.

There were little monkeys in the new cage.

The zoo was beautiful.
All the animals made it beautiful
And the grass, too.

USING THE KEY VOCABULARY APPROACH

Key Vocabulary is a technique developed by Sylvia Ashton War-ner, working with very young Maori Indian children in New Zealand, as a means of bridging the gap between talking, reading, and writing. Warner refers to the process as an "organic approach." She believes the child brings to school with him thousands of words that "represent the inner self," words to express fears, loves, desires, and hates. She contends that the teacher should reach into the child's mind to find these words that have intrinsic meaning to him and then use them as a natural bridge to reading.[7]

Jeannette Veatch, well known authority on individualized reading instruction, became interested in the approach and directed what was called "Prebook Reading—Key Vocabulary Study." A team of educa-tors, Sawiki, Barnette, Blakey, and Elliot, worked with Veatch to refine and further develop the study over a three year period in working with first and second grade children. In the words of the developers:

> Key vocabulary makes it possible to zero in on the child as a per-son and to nourish each child's feelings and thoughts. . . . The child

---

[7]Sylvia Ashton Warner, *Teacher* (New York: Simon and Schuster, 1963).

becomes self-directed and the teacher's role is reversed. She is no longer a supplier of "information" but rather, a facilitator of learning.[8]

The basic steps as found in the Key Vocabulary guide are outlined as follows:

1. The child gives to the teacher his "best word"—one that has emotional impact for him.
2. He whispers the word into the teacher's ear—it adds intrigue but is also a security factor. Later the whisper technique will be discarded.
3. The teacher writes the word on a 3½ x 11 inch card with a felt pen. The child names the letters he knows.
4. The child traces the word with his finger.
5. The child does something with his word—he may write it, draw a picture of it, write it on the chalkboard, or write other "words" about his word.
6. The next day, the word is reviewed. The words the child does not know are discarded. Only those remembered will have significance.

Veatch states, "I have always felt this practice to be an initiating step into an extensive program dependent upon children's own talk written down."[9] The practice, in use in many classrooms in Arizona, holds particular promise for youngsters who are learning English as a second language. The limitations of the language experience approach cited earlier can be partly met by beginning with this one-word, one-concept approach. The full program is offered in the text.

FROM DICTATION TO CREATIVE WRITING

Creative writing begins on a simple scale. It may be a single word under a picture, a simple phrase above a painting, or a complicated philosophic observation such as the one written by Ricky.[10]

---

[8]Jeannette Veatch, Eleanor Barnette, Janice Blakey, Geraldine Elliot, and Florence Sawiki, *Key Words to Reading: The Language Experience Approach Begins* (Columbus, Ohio: Charles E. Merrill Publishing Co., 1973).

[9]Ibid.

[10]The creative stories which follow were written by members of Mrs. Marietta Coffin's class at Grand Avenue School in Phoenix, Arizona.

When I Am Seven
I am good be kuus I am seven.
Seven is very good uou know.
Seven is the best time.
          Ricky

Doug reflected on "Being Five." While the structure was less pol-
ished, the story was full of action.

When I was 5 i was trubel.
And sometims i was very bad to.
So she gives me a spking and
it was not good. So i tryed to
be good. And Now I AM GOOD.

Steve expressed his Thanksgiving thoughts by writing:

I love my Mother and Brother and
Father and Pat and God and
everything like American and the
whole wide world becaus God makes it.

Five year old Kimberli wrote in a different form with every word
spelled correctly:

That's that!
Did you ever see a fat cat?
Did you ever see a chair with hair?
Did you ever see a lake break?
Did you ever see a snail sail?
Did you ever hear some dirt burp?

The story written by seven year old Tony, after a long and troubled
session with paper and pencil, probably represents the ultimate in creative effort.

I am trying to think of something to
rite. I can't think of anything to rite. I mite think
of something to rite but if I do, I hope its better
than what I just rote.

With only two words to change, Tony's effort appeared in the class booklet for all to read. Tony made the change, *not* his teacher.

Group Dictation

In the brief time it takes to ask a question, it is possible to direct students' attention toward a "happening" and then record emotional reactions. A sudden rain shower might serve to illustrate the point.

With faces pressed hard against window panes, reactions are spontaneous. Written on chalkboard or chart, the comments represent meaningful content for a "talk-read" experience.

> makes me scared
> makes me cold
> looks like a river
> sound like a drum
> giving the tree a bath.

CONCEPTS GROW AS STUDENTS LISTEN, OBSERVE, PERCEIVE RELATIONSHIPS AND THEN REACT

At first, learning experiences are very informal, focusing heavily on direct observation, first hand participation, and guided conversation. The classroom, particularly for bilingual situations, may resemble the local "Variety Store." Concrete objects serve as references for language growth. The child accumulates oral vocabulary as he experiments with speech in real-life situations.

Our Guppies

First we had two guppies. Now we have a whole bunch.

We capitalize on transitory interests; pets, toys, insects, unexpected events, a sudden storm with hailstones bombarding classroom windows.

With chalk in hand, the teacher can convert oral language to symbolic language by simply recording what students have observed or experienced.

Stories are dictated by groups in the form of charts. Simple ones at first, about a surprise, a plan, a rhyme, a riddle, or a happening.

The chart tells the story of a shared activity. As the teacher writes on a transparency, children watch the projected image on a screen. Visual acuity is sharpened as each letter takes form.

Capturing the Magic Moment

The praying mantis egg case has been on the science table for a week—just a dry pouch on a dry branch. But today something is happening. Tiny insects are bursting from the case, only a few at first, then dozens of them flying from tables to desks and desks to children.

This is no time for story hour regardless of the day's schedule. It is a magic moment for learning, rich with promise. The stage is set for conversation, questions, and interaction:

> I wonder what a praying mantis eats?
> How many were in the egg case?
> How long will these insects live?
> Are they harmful or are they helpful?

Lets find out!—an open invitation for students to *inquire, observe,* and *share.* It's a time for books, pictures, and charts. It's a time for discovery. The situation lends itself to a group experience story. After the observation, the teacher can develop a simple chart recording the students' reaction. The teacher directs the discussion:

> "We had some very strange visitors today. Now they have all gone away. But we could write a story about them. What shall we name our story? Yes, we could say, *Our Funny Visitors.* Watch as I write it. Now, what do you want me to write about our funny visitors?"

By guiding responses through questions, the teacher can elicit from the students three, four, perhaps five sentences. The completed story might develop as follows:

Our Funny Visitors
We had a surprise today.
The praying mantis hatched.
They flew all over the room.
They look hungry.

The experience story served four general purposes:

1. It introduced reading as talk written down.
2. It oriented the students in left-to-right progression across the page.
3. It introduced a number of words which will be utilized again and again as high utility sight words.
4. Letter-sound relationships were stressed as the teacher pronounced and wrote each word simultaneously.

INITIATING PROBLEM-CENTERED READING

The teacher threads substance and content into the primary curriculum by designing spirals of experience around a core of social living and science concepts. Observation, listening, speaking, and reading are synchronized as learning experiences are focused on concerns of the environment. At primary levels those concerns gradually expand (1) from self to others, (2) from home to school, (3) from neighborhood to community, and (4) from the immediate environment to the wider world of living things and physical phenomena.

The primary child is initiated into problem-centered learning as he engages in unit type activities centered around concepts:

1. about self (pets, friends, toys, personal experiences).
2. about family (mother, father, siblings, role of family members, social life, customs).

3. about the immediate environment (neighborhood, food, clothing, shelter).
4. about current happenings in school, at home and in the community.
5. about the community (workers, community needs, safety and protection, transportation, communication, customs, holidays).
6. about the living world (plants, animals, insects, etc.).
7. about the physical world (land and water, weather and climate, seasons of the year, natural resources).

Specialized Reading Skills

Differentiated thinking skills are employed as children investigate, discuss, make generalizations, draw conclusions, and put their ideas to work. Such activities as planning with other children, sharing ideas, dramatizing, viewing films, experiencing through field trips, and using reading resources to solve problems contribute to the development of higher levels of thinking demanded in content reading.

Those specialized reading-thinking skills of deep concern to the teacher of primary children are:

1. the ability to form and to store clear mental images from sensory input.
2. the ability to perceive relationships of time, space, sequence, cause and effect.
3. the ability to organize fragmentary thinking into logical ideas.
4. the ability to mentally edit and then restate what is heard or what is read.
5. the ability to make reasonable predictions based on judgments of facts given.
6. the ability to differentiate between fantasy and fact.

Child-Centered Content

It is through unit type activities that the teacher can implement the language experience approach to best advantage. Charts, records, daily logs, dictated stories, individual creative writing, class newspapers, booklets, teacher-composed materials, and many other forms of writing are put to use as students engage in relevant problem solving tasks.

Social studies and science textbooks give direction and serve as valuable sources of information, particularly because of selected pictures and illustrations. At early primary grade levels, however, vocabulary limitations restrict the content. Usually a science or social studies textbook, at first grade level, offers one-sentence captions under pictures or employs simple narrative stories to develop a concept. Much of the content may be irrelevant to the lives of culture-different children. Actually, it would be virtually impossible to produce social studies textbooks that focus on local needs due to the divergence in cultural, linguistic, and historical backgrounds.

Later in primary levels, the language-culture-different child will be better prepared to make use of content-centered texts, but in the first and second grades, the teacher must rely heavily on content that emerges from on-going activities.

IMPLEMENTING EXPERIENCE-WRITING IN SOCIAL LIVING ACTIVITIES

New Language Concepts from a First-hand Experience

A primary class visited a dairy, bought whole milk, skimmed off the cream and churned it. They extracted the butterfat from the buttermilk, weighted the butter and finally served it on crackers to visiting parents. Out of this meaningful segment of a social studies unit came new concepts and a fund of new words.

An evaluation of the activity revealed that children had used the following words in their creative writing related to the unit: *churn, separate, whole, skimmed, homogenized, pasteurized, degrees, butterfat, buttermilk, dairy, beef, ounce, pound, quart, pint* and *gallon.*

Those words will not appear in a primer, a first grade book, and perhaps not in a third grade reader. Yet they represented high utility words for this particular group. Chances are, all will be remembered.

Specialized Vocabulary from a Field Trip

A Vegetable Farm

We went to see a vegetable farm. We saw many plants that give us food. We bought vegetables for a salad. We will make a salad for our lunch.

Recording the children's report of a shared experience is an application of all the facets of communication—listening, speaking, writing and reading.

From the chart, which will be read and reread, will come many new words. Some will be selected as sight words. Some will serve individual writing needs. High utility words will be placed on flash cards and filed alphabetically in the class word file.

Words We Need

Farm	we	went	for	good
plant	our	give	to	many
food	us	saw	that	
lunch		make	A	
		a		

Words I Need

Each child will select the words he needs and place them in his individual word file or in an individual dictionary.

Classroom News Writing

Producing a classroom newspaper provides an excellent means of involving children in a personalized writing-reading experience. It fulfills an important reading objective—reading for information. It gives legitimate reason for correct usage and responsible writing. It is a way to motivate children to write, whether their contribution is a simple, single line under a drawing, a dictated news item, or an original article.

At beginning levels, *The Daily News* may be no more than a bulletin board or a single sheet printed and shared with parents and other classes.

The Daily News

Today's News	School News	Notices	Lost and Found
In the World			
		Stories	
In Our Town			

Colored yarn separates the columns and can be adjusted to accommodate spaces needed for news stories, notices, lost and found items, jokes, original poems and stories as well as cartoons.

By mid-year, a class might decide that the newspaper should be dittoed and distributed to family and friends.

LESSON PLAN
BUILT AROUND A SCIENCE CONCEPT

Objectives	Activities	Materials
Concepts	**Large Group Activity**	**Materials and Aids**
All animals are alike in some way.	All students participate in observation-discussion centered on a live turtle.	1. Live turtle
All animals are different in some way.		2. Food for turtle
		3. Oak tag chart paper
Some animals live only on land.	**1. Total Group Activity** Guided discussion: Sequence of questions designed to lead students to make discoveries about the turtle.	4. Pictures of different types of turtles
Some live only in the water.		5. Poem: "Talking to a Turtle"
Turtles can live on land or in water.		6. *Science for a Changing World;* Book I, B. John Syrocki & Theodore Munch, Chicago: Benefic Press, 1967, pp. 108–125.
Turtles are reptiles.	**2. Small Group Activity** One teacher classroom: One group develops an experience story while others draw pictures of the turtle. Groups alternate.	
Skill Development Students should be able to:		**Evaluation** Individual responses will be used as a means of evaluating language-concept development.
a. express understandings related to the above concepts.	**3. Team Teaching** Class divided into small groups under direction of teachers and aides to develop experience stories.	
b. contribute to the development of a dictated experience chart.		**Work sheet** Will be used to check word recognition; Students will match words in column I with words in column II
c. dictate a sentence reflecting an observation made.	**4. Individual Activity** Each student draws, paints, or colors a picture.	
d. accurately match sentence and phrase strips to sentences and phrases on the experience chart.	**5. Directed Reading Activity** Match sentence strips. Match phrases. (description of activity follows.)	bug — Turtle pet — shell shell — bug turtle — pet eats — hides catch — eats hides — catch funny — Big big — Funny

UTILIZING THE LANGUAGE EXPERIENCE APPROACH IN A SCIENCE ACTIVITY

The content areas provide a means of making transitions from informal language activity to more highly organized learning experiences. Through observation and discussion, content emerges in the form of experience charts and experience writing. In the lesson plan below activities are built around a science concept appropriate to early primary levels.

This plan briefly outlines concepts, objectives, and general procedures. Following is an elaboration of the strategies involved:

Procedure:

Seat students in a circle on the floor where all can watch a live turtle. Provide suitable food, a tub of water, and room for the turtle to crawl. Students should be allowed to handle the turtle and observe his actions both in and out of the water.

Guided Discussion:

(Questioning strategies are directed toward specific levels of thinking in relation to concepts involved.)

Making Associations:

Where do you think a turtle might live? Where could we go to find another turtle just like this one? Does this turtle make you think of any other animal you have ever seen? Why? Does he move as fast as a frog? As slow as a snail? Watch him crawl. Does that give you an idea of a name for him?

Making Comparisons:

Is our turtle more like a squirrel or a frog? Is he more like a frog or a snail? Is he more like a snail or a snake?

Perceiving Relationships:

In what way is the turtle like a snail? How is he different? In what way is he like a snake? What do snakes eat? What did our turtle eat? Can a snake live in the water? Can the turtle swim in water? Can they both live on land and in water? What is a reptile?

Drawing Conclusions:

How do you protect yourself? Tell us how *your pet* protects himself.

How do you suppose our turtle protects himself? Why does he need a shell?

Generalizing:

Would you want a turtle for a pet? Why or why not? Do turtles help us? How? Could a turtle live in the ocean? Could a turtle live in the desert? In what way are all animals alike?

Composing an
Experience Chart

Our Pet Turtle

Our turtle eats bugs.
He has a hard shell.
He hides in his shell.
We'll catch some big bugs for
   him.
He likes flies and bugs.
And mosquitos too!
He's a funny pet.

Immediately following the observation-discussion, an experience chart is developed.

Step 1

Teacher: "What shall we name our story? What shall we tell first? What does he like to eat?"

Through questioning, the teacher elicits responses, then writes directly from dictation. The chart typifies possible responses. In beginning charts, each sentence is treated as a complete paragraph and is written in paragraph form as shown in line five.

Step 2—Re-reading:

Teacher: "Find the sentence that tells where he hides." "Come up and frame it with your hands." "Tell us what it says." "Now frame the part that tells what we will catch for our turtle." "Yes, some big bugs." (Procedure continues until all sentences are re-read.)

Step 3—Reinforcement:

The teacher should prepare two copies of the chart; one to be left on a bulletin board within reach of the students, the other to be cut into sentence strips. The strips are placed randomly on a pocket chart beside the bulletin board. Children match sentence strips to the master chart.

Step 4—Phrase study:

Sentence strips are cut into phrase units, for example:

| Our turtle | in his shell | he hides | eats bugs |

Students match phrase cards to identical phrases on the master chart, first reading the phrase, then the complete sentence. Example: Child: "This says, *in his shell.* It belongs on this sentence. It says, *He hides in his shell.*"

Step 5—Word study:

Phrase strips are cut into word cards. These words, selected by teacher and students, may be placed on charts along with the cumulative sight words from other activities.

Naming Words		Word to Describe Things	Action Words	Helpers
turtle	Our	hard	eats	is
bugs	he	funny	hides	has
shell	He	big	catch	and
pet	him		likes	for

Extended Activities

It will be possible for many of the students to write and illustrate an original story about the turtle. Library books about turtles should be available for all.

LITERARY READING

Above all, reading should be a pleasurable experience. The highest possible goal for any reading program should be that children will read because they like to read and that they will continue to enjoy reading throughout their lifetime.

Children probably first sense the joy and satisfaction of reading through rhymes and make-believe tales. "The Three Bears" may well be the motivational force that leads hundreds of children to and through the first grade reader, to *Rabbit Hill,* to *Charlotte's Web,* to *Johnny Tremain,* to *20,000 Leagues Under the Sea,* and on, and on, and on. To leave to chance the possibility that a child will eventually discover the enchantment of books is to overlook the entire purpose of reading instruction. Providing built-in time for exposure to literary experience is just as important as providing time for skill instruction.

Listening to Stories

Literary sensitivity is nutured through hearing language used powerfully. It begins at home, when parents read to their children. Preferably, it should begin before the infant can talk. Hearing the rhythm of language through rhymes, and songs, and the repetitive lines of nursery tales, tunes the ear to the melody of speech. But many, many children do not have such preschool experiences.

For those children who have not grown up with books (and for those who have) there must be time set aside for listening to the teacher read. Taped stories read by men's voices as well as women's should be used to extend such opportunities. "Talking books" complete with taped cassettes allow the child to follow along as he sits at a listening center.

Using Literary Experiences to Improve Language Proficiency

There have been a number of important innovative projects utilizing literary experiences as a means of raising proficiency in written and oral English. Wasserman[11] conducted a program with Mexican-American children from a disadvantaged area, using literature as a springboard for composition and other language explorations. Bumpas[12] used the repetitious lines of the old familiar tales told to children as models for teaching young students English as a foreign language.

In the Wasserman project, selection from folk tales, fanciful stories, adventure, myths, and fables were used as model stories. Children were made aware of motifs found to be common in such selections. Basically the motifs followed a pattern found in such stories as *The Three Billy Goats Gruff* or the *Gingerbread Boy*. Teachers involved students in many listening-speaking activities through which they heard and used the repetitive lines of the selection again and again. After total familiarity with the story, the teacher elicited from students the motif of the model story. Then as a group, the students composed a story, in their personal language, incorporating the motif but originating new characters and new dialogue. Results were exciting stories such as one about a Tortilla who said, "I ran away from a little old woman. I ran away from a little old man and I can run away from you, I can."

As a result of the project, Wasserman drew the following conclusion:

> Literature appears to provide a wealth of some of the finest language upon which children can build their own understandings of English and extend their own personal language.

---

[11]Susan Wasserman, "Raising the English Language Proficiency of Mexican-American Children in the Primary Grades," *California English Journal*, April, 1970, pp. 22–27.

[12]Faye L. Bumpas, *Teaching Young Students English as a Foreign Language* (New York: American Book Company, 1963).

Children do internalize the language they hear if they are provided with many opportunities for hearing and utilizing language.[12]

Planned Time for Personal Reading

The classroom library must offer a wide choice of reading materials. A center, attractively arranged, in a carpeted area, is an open invitation to read. If books are color coded with a strip of tape to indicate levels of difficulty, students soon discover which books they can read and understand.

It is critically important to program times for all children to do self-selected reading. If library reading is viewed as a reward for completing work on time, or a spare time activity, the child who needs it most is often deprived of the opportunity. The student who comes from an economically deprived background needs time to live with books in the classroom.

Some teachers make arrangements for older children from other classes to read stories to primary children or to listen to children read for them. Tutorial reading with a student buddy can benefit both parties involved.

Culture-Oriented Materials

Currently, many new materials are available to acquaint children with the cultural contributions of Mexican-Americans and American Indians. Interesting books about blacks who have contributed to the American way of life are appearing on the market written on a level appropriate for young children.

Particularly exciting are the culturally oriented materials being developed *by children for children* to read. A good example of such materials is the series, *Culture and History Oriented Materials*[14], written and illustrated by teachers and students at the Gila River Community Schools at Sacaton, Arizona.

A book entitled *The Skunk,* composed and dictated to the teacher by first grade students living on an Indian reservation, is typical of materials developed by children for others to read. Pages from that book reveal creative ability of the young writers and artists. Equally as vivid is another entitled, *The Coyote.*

---

[13]Wasserman, p. 27.

[14]*Culture and History Oriented Materials,* produced by University of Arizona Research and Services, Sacaton Project, in cooperation with the Bureau of Indian Affairs, Pima Agency, Branch of Education, John R. O'Brien, Administrator.

The Skunk

Skunks eat insects.

The skunk is nocturnal.
He travel at night.

A skunk can make
a bad smell.

He has a squirt gun.

A complete series, grades one through eight, was developed on the legends of the Pima Indian People.[15] Children asked parents or grandparents to tell them the old tales and legends of the Pima tribe. The students retold the legends to teachers who edited and typed them for publication. The stories appear now in booklet form, with full illustrations by the students. Titles such as "Lightening of the Sky," "Why the Coyote Looks Back," "The Pima Challenge," and "The Great Star Man" indicate the type of material developed. The consultant coordinator, Dorothy Piercey, prepared glossaries to aid the reader and teacher.

The materials are checked out by students as self-choice reading materials. The project served to stimulate a great deal of interest among students and parents, as well as to create a great deal of community interest.

EXTENDED READINGS

Barrett, Thomas C. "Visual Discrimination Tasks as Predictors of First Grade Reading Achievement." *Reading Teacher* (January 1965): 273–276.

Binnie, C., D. Elkind, and J. Steward. "A Comparison of the Visual Perceptual Abilities of Acoustically Impaired and Hearing Children." *International Audiology* 5 (1966):233–241.

Beyer, Evelyn. "Language Learning-Fresh Vivid and Their Own." *Childhood Education* 48, no. 1 (October 1971): 21–24.

De Hirsch, Katrina, J. Jeanette Jansky, and William S. Langford. *Preventing Reading Failure.* New York: Harper and Row, 1967.

Deutch, Martin. "The Disadvantaged Child and the Learning Process." *Education in Depressed Areas.* New York: Bureau of Publications, Teachers College, Columbia University, 1963.

Durkin, Delores. *Teaching Young Children to Read.* Boston: Allyn and Bacon, Inc., 1972, pp. 63–112.

Dykstra, Robert. "Auditory Discrimination Abilities and Beginning Reading Achievement," *Reading Research Quarterly* 1 (Spring 1966):32.

Hillerick, Robert L. "Pre-reading Skills in Kindergarten: A Second Report." *Elementary School Journal* 65 (March 1965):312–317.

Hodges, Richard E. and Hugh E. Rudorf, eds. *Language and Learning to Read.* Boston: Houghton Mifflin Company, 1972. Chapters Two, Three, and Five.

[15]*Indian Legend Series,* written and illustrated by elementary students of Sacaton Schools, produced by Bureau of Research and Services, Arizona State University at Tempe, in cooperation with the Bureau of Indian Affairs, Pima Agency.

Kunz, Jean T. "The Self-Concept of the Young Child as He Learns to Read." in *Readings on Teaching Reading,* ed. Sam Leaton Sebasta and Carl J. Wallen. Chicago: Science Research Associates, Inc. 1972.

Sebasta, Sam Leaton and Carl J. Wallen, *The First R: Readings on Teaching Reading,* Chicago: Science Research Associates, Inc. 1972. Chapter two.

Wattenberg, W. W. and C. Clifford. *Relationship of the Self-Concept to Beginning Achievement in Reading.* Project of Office of Education, United States Department of Health, Education and Welfare. Detroit, Michigan: Wayne State University, 1962.

Wepman, Joseph M. "Auditory Discrimination, Speech and Reading." *Elementary School Journal* (March 1960):325–333.

CHAPTER 7

Building
Basic Skills

Five basic objectives are critical in regard to the child's vocabulary power. If the child is progressing satisfactorily in this strand of the basic reading skills, he demonstrates the following:

1. He is accumulating a fund of sight words that he recognizes instantly.
2. He is developing skill in coding speech sounds to written symbols.
3. He is becoming proficient in using phonological clues to unlock new words.
4. He is using language structures as clues to vocabulary meanings.
5. He is developing the ability to encode speech sounds into symbols as he writes.

PART I

Vocabulary Power

There are many avenues through which the student may develop vocabulary power. There is no doubt that television, advertising and other forms of mass media in the "outside school" environment are powerful forces influencing children's vocabularies. *Sesame Street, The Electric Company, Captain Kangaroo,* as well as *Bugs Bunny, Dr. Doolittle,* and *Scooby Doo* occupy hours of the child's time away from the classroom. Research is very much needed to investigate the effect that present day television programs are having on the size of children's vocabularies.

Strategies designed to build vocabulary power in the primary classroom must include both systematic skill instruction and a variety of opportunities for the student to build his personal vocabulary. Toward that effort teachers must maintain a balance in skill instruction.

Opportunities for acquiring sight words should include three major avenues:

From teacher directed language experiences	Sight Words	From the controlled vocabulary introduced through basal readers
	From Individualized Writing Experiences	

A systematic program of instruction should provide experiences for students to discover sound patterns and structure patterns.

From a linguistic base where sound patterns and structure patterns are discovered	Vocabulary Power	From multi-sensory experiences where auditory, visual and tactile experiences are employed.

Three Types of Vocabulary

If there were a one-to-one correspondence between letters and sounds, the decoding system would be relatively simple. The child would learn the sound, apply the rule, and then drill for mastery. Since many words have irregular spellings, the student must have diverse ways of attacking unknown words. In reality there are three different types of words the child encounters in his early reading experiences:

1. Words that conform to regular spelling patterns that can be decoded.
2. Words that have irregular spelling patterns that do not conform to rules or generalizations.
3. Words that occur infrequently, but serve temporary needs.

A systematic program of instruction must be carried out to enable the student to deal with all three types.

Phonetic Analysis

Studies indicate that reading instruction which includes strong emphasis on phonics does result in higher achievement at the end of grade one than programs which place little emphasis on phonic instruction.[1] We have long since passed through the "no phonics era." The fuss over phonics that continues to perplex educators is centered on *how* phonics should be taught, not *why*.

A significant number of monosyllabic words appearing in reading texts and other materials used at early primary levels do conform to regular spelling patterns. These patterns serve as clues to pronunciation and therefore are decodable. The vowel-consonant (V-C) patterns are indicated in the following:

1. Words that conform to long and short vowel sound patterns:

CVC	VC	CV	CVC$_e$	CVVC
men	at	me	cape	peel
pat	it	so	made	wait
zip	up	he	late	read
that	on	snow	grade	coat

2. Words that do not conform to long and short vowel sound patterns:

CVC	VC	CV	CVC$_e$	CVVC
put	oh	to	have	sieve
tall	or	do	come	believe
far		who	share	said
won			caste	boil

What we have said, of course, is that in spite of the lack of correspondence between sounds and letters, English does have a phonological system. It is predictable to the degree that many words can be decoded on the basis of the vowel-constant patterns such as shown above, and on the basis of structure patterns dealing with roots, endings, prefixes and suffixes. We believe children can use these patterns to unlock words. We believe that they learn how to use them through a discovery approach as they manipulate language rather than through learning rules that have less than 70 to 80 percent applicability.

---

[1]Arthur W. Heilman, *Principles and Practices of Teaching Reading* (Columbus, Ohio: Charles E. Merrill Publishing Co., 1972), p. 239.

Regardless of the strategy used, the objective is clear-cut. The student must become proficient in acquiring new vocabulary on his own. That means he must develop a systematic "sounding out" system as well as to become something of a "super-sleuth" in recognizing and using clues available in the structures of language.

Structural Analysis

There is no sharp distinction between phonetic analysis and structural analysis. It is difficult to know whether a child is relying upon visual or auditory clues as he unlocks words. For example, in unlocking the word *unlikely,* the child may be using the *ly* as an adverb marker, the *un* as a structure clue for a prefix, the *ike* as a spelling pattern clue, or the *like* as a root word. Our hope is that he will be versatile in his attack. Indeed, one of the teacher's chief aims in teaching word-analysis abilities is to have pupils gain skill in combining several approaches in word study. In a practical situation, accordingly, the problem is not one of phonetic analysis versus structural analysis but the best combined method of word attack.

Mature readers automatically rely on many structure clues that are built-in characteristics of English. Children can be alerted to these clues from the first. Actually, the structure system of English is more reliable than the phonological system. Second language learners particularly should be taught how to use the system as an aid to word recognition.

The following examples indicate how language structures serve as clues to word recognition:

Syntactical Clues

Once _____ _____ _____.
I'll go up the l_____.
One, two, _____.
"Help me," _____ Tom.
_____ apples are _____.

Form Class Markers

The rain fell _____ly.
He was _____ing his horse.
I like p_____es and cream.
Many l_____ies came.

.

TEACHING PHONICS THROUGH A
SOUND-TO-SYMBOL APPROACH

A child learns to speak by listening and observing. His speaking vocabulary grows as he imitates his parents and his peers. By experimentation his babbling becomes more organized. It would seem reasonable that the reading vocabulary might be acquired in the same way.

Bridging the Gap Between the Listening-Speaking
Vocabulary and the Reading-Writing
Vocabulary

Listen

Listen and Say

Say and Look

Look, Read, and Build

From the listening speaking-vocabulary	To the reading-writing vocabulary

The second language learner needs a great deal of support as he attempts to "crack the code" of English. There are two ways to approach the teaching of letter-sound relationships. One way is to present letters or combinations of letters and then tell the student what sound these letters make. The process is prescriptive. Rote memory may be involved. The other approach reverses the process. The child begins with his own speech sounds. He is led to discover that those sounds can be represented by letters. The latter approach, based on the notion that writing simply represents speech, is descriptive. The process is inductive.

At the risk of over-simplification, the following example illustrates the rationale behind the sound-to-symbol approach:

Listen: "boy," "Bob," "best" (teacher pronounces)

Listen and Say: "You say a word that begins the same way." (student responds)

Say and Look: (Teacher pronounces as she writes "boy," "Bob," "best." Student traces forms in air while repeating words.)

Look, Read, and Build: Teacher: "boy," "Bob" "You read the words." "Look, b___, B___. You write a word that begins like this."

Implementing the Sound-to-Symbol Approach

The following sequence of activities is intended to show the process involved in the sound-to-symbol approach. The activities merely suggest possibilities for implementation. There are countless ways of working with word elements:

A SOUND TO SYMBOL ACTIVITY

1. Patterns Introduced:

   phoneme *b*
   spelling pattern *ug*
   sentence pattern:
   I saw a _____.

2. Auditory Stimulus:

   Teacher: "Listen:
   "*bug.*"
   "Look"
   "You say, *bug*"
   (Students respond)
   Teacher: "I saw a bug under a rock.
   Where did you see a bug?"
   (Students respond; ex: "I saw a bug on leaf.")

3. Tactile Stimulus:

   Teacher: "Listen and watch my lips: *big, bug, beetle.*"
   Show labial (lip) position for plosive *b*.
   Teacher: "You say *bug, beetle*. Tell me another word that begins like bug."

4. Visual Stimulus:

   Teacher (using picture clues):

   "Find a picture that begins the same way as bug. Put a circle around each thing that begins the same way."

5. Tactile (trace):

   Teacher: "Look, this word is *bug*." (Word on board)
   "Write it in the air. This is the letter *b*. Write it in the air."

6. Sound-symbol Substitution:

   Teacher: "Listen: *bug, dug.*"
   "Look," (a chart)

   > A Bug!
   > A bug, a bug!
   > I dug and dug.
   > I found a bug.
   > -ug! -ug!

   Students: (Read, then frame words *dug, bug, ug.*)
   Teacher: "Write *bug*. Take off the *b*. Make your word say (*dug*), (*tug*), (*jug*.)"
   (t, j, d previously presented.)

7. Oral Sentence Context Clues:

   Teacher: "I have a dog with a funny turned up nose. I call him _____, yes, Pug. You write *Pug*. Sometimes he likes to curl up snug as a bug in a _____, yes, rug. You write *rug*."

8. Spelling Pattern Chaining
   The Ladder Game
   Spelling pattern *ug*.

t	ug						
b	ug	l	ug	dr	ug	th	ug
d	ug	j	ug	sn	ug	sh	ug
p	ug	r	ug				

Evaluation:

Seat Work   You write:

   Is it a bug? yes no   It's a _____.
   Is it a jug? yes no   It's a _____.
   Is it a bug? yes no   It's a _____.

BUILDING VOCABULARY POWER THROUGH LANGUAGE PATTERNS

Learning How Words Work

If we apply linguistic principles to reading instruction, we begin at primary levels to help children discover how words work. We provide situations through which words are used in functional writing: as (1) namers, (2) activators, (3) describers, (4) qualifiers, and (5) service words.

Classifying Words

Some teachers use vocabulary charts as a means of developing word classifications. From the very beginning, as high utility words are encountered in writing, they are placed on the charts for continuous reference. In a sense, such open-ended word charts become a classroom dictionary.

If the charts are color-coded, reference usage is increased and there is possibility for association with word classes. For example, the namers (nouns) can be placed on red chart paper, activators (verbs) on green, describers (adjectives) on yellow, and qualifiers (adverbs) on blue. If flash cards and dictionary cards are also color-coded, there is reinforcement of the function aspect of words.

Naming Words

Charts can be designed to fit needs as they are encountered:

Some Words Name Things to Eat and Drink

1. carrots	1. grapes	1. cake	1. milk
2. cabbage	2. pears	2. bread	2. water
3. tomatoes	3. apples	3. pancakes	3. juice
4. onions	4. bananas	4. biscuits	4. malted milk

Similarly, charts could be constructed to list: (1) Things to Wear, (2) Places to Visit, (3) Things to Buy in a Hardware Store, (4) Things to See in the City, etc.

How Words Work Together

The following charts suggest ways in which students can discover how some words pattern with others. Attached to each chart are pockets containing "partner words" that function with each category. As the student manipulates the partner word by placing it before the words on the chart, he not only discovers how words work together for meaning but is learning sight words.

1. Words to Name
   Things
   __turtle
   __car
   __house

2. Words to Name
   People
   __father   __girl
   __mother   __baby
   __boy   __teacher

3. Words to Name
   Places
   __home   __farm
   __school   __city
   __store   __birdhouse

A student will soon discover that he can build (expand) the namer word by adding both a signaler (a, an, or the) and a describer. For example: a turtle, a big turtle, some big turtle, or the birdhouse, the old birdhouse, the funny old birdhouse.

*Words to Tell What
We Do or Did*

hop:	hopping	hopped
look:	looking	looked
walk:	walking	walked
help:	helping	helped

The function of endings is discovered when the student learns he can pattern *are, is, was* and *were* with words ending in *ing* but not with words ending in *ed*. Example: *is hopping, was hopping,* but not *is hopped, was hopped.*

Words for Work Tasks

The creative teacher will find ways to help students discover how words work through on-going activities. (If there is a predominant "other language," a bilingual approach can be used.)

A great many words come from gardening activities. Room charts tell the story.

Words for Work in our Garden		Words for Plants in our Garden	
dig	(escavar)	radishes	(robano)
pull	(extraer)	onions	(cebolla)
plant	(planta)	carrots	(zanahoria)
cultivate	(cultivar)	lettuce	(lechuga)
irrigate	(irrigacion)	weeds	(hierba)

Work for Today
Pull weeds—Stanley
           Barbara
Dig carrots—Josie
           Eddie
Pick lettuce—Juanito
           Mary
Pull onions—Jeffery
Wash the   Sara
vegetables—Tony
Make the Salad—Everyone!

A Surprise
Guess what happened!
A little grey rabbit was in our garden.
He ate our lettuce.
He nibbled our carrots.
He will come back again, we think.
What shall we do?

PART II

BASIC SKILL DEVELOPMENT THROUGH
BASAL READING SERIES

As a result of nationwide concern and public interest in reading in the past few years, a great many new programs have emerged in the form of published textbook series, programmed reading instruction materials, and audio-visual materials. Some hint of old methods with new titles, some reflect bold new approaches, and some simply represent an experimental effort.

Basically, most of the current materials and published programs appear to fall into the following general categories:

1. Comprehensive basal readers
2. Content-oriented basal reading series
3. Programmed reading materials
4. Language experience based reading materials
5. Linguistically oriented reading series

The influence of linguists in reading methodology in recent years is reflected in new terms such as:

1. Phonemic reading approaches
2. Phonemic-pronounciation approaches
3. Psycho-linguistic approaches
4. Coding approaches

The expanding textbook market, particularly in light of federally funded reading programs for disadvantaged students, has enticed many writers to produce new materials. The teacher of language-different, culture-different children must evaluate rather carefully the offerings available.

The first step would be to determine which approach to reading makes most sense in relation to the teacher's experience, level of expertise, and point of view about reading instruction. No plan will work unless the teacher is convinced of its reliability, enthusiastic about the program, and competent in implementing it. The second step is to examine the advantages and disadvantages of each approach in light of the school's policy, the availability of materials, and the nature of the school's organizational plan. The third step, and the most important, is to determine which approach appears to be most appropriate to the needs of the particular students within the class group.

Comprehensive Basal Reader Series

Publishers of basal reading programs offer a series of student texts made up of selections of stories, poems, and other literary or informative content.

The content, often organized in unit form, provides the student with a sequential series of reading experiences.

The teacher's edition for each student text provides a plan for implementing the skills of comprehension, vocabulary development and word recognition. Each lesson plan outlines procedures for guiding the student through a series of sequential learning activities in these areas.

An examination of a teacher's edition of most series will reveal that basic skill development provides for (1) silent reading skills, (2) oral reading skills, (3) comprehension abilities, (4) critical thinking skills, (5) vocabulary growth, (6) word recognition skills, and (7) suggestions for extending reading experiences. Many of the newly published series include activities for building linguistic skills. Some include specific provision for assessing reading levels, and diagnosing reading difficulties.

Advantages of a Comprehensive Basal Reader Program

Most text series offer:

1. An orderly sequence of skill building.
2. A defined plan of action for developing and extending these skills.
3. Content that is geared to grade level areas and controlled in vocabulary and concept level.
4. A variety of content that usually includes a balance between real life and make-believe stories, between literary selections and content-oriented material, and between prose and poetry.

Possible Limitations of a Basal Reader Program

1. Content of some basal readers is aimed only toward middle class anglo-oriented social settings.
2. Content may be irrelevant to the local geographic environment and the experiential background and values of the students.
3. Speech patterns used in the content may be couched in a style unlike the child's speech repertoire.
4. Vocabulary control may "water down" content to the point that it has low interest appeal for many students.
5. Basal readers may fail to provide for individual differences among students within the group.

Questions, Pro and Con

1. Is it possible that the basal program offers a foundational support in sequential skill building that may otherwise become a hodgepodge of fragmentary activities?

2. Does the basal program serve to alleviate some of the time pressures in an already overcrowded curriculum?
3. Is it possible that creative teachers can overcome the lack of relevancy to the student's environment by creative discussion and intelligent use of the materials?
4. Is it possible that many of the criticisms of basal readers are inherent in abuses of basal reader programs?
5. Is selectivity the key to the problem; i.e., *which basal program, for which group of students, for how long, and under what condition?*
6. Is it true that some basal programs are totally irrelevant to a particular socio-ethnic group and should not be used?
7. Does the vocabulary control of some readers so stultify the content that it turns off children's interest?
8. Do basal reader programs fail to provide for the wide range of abilities, interests and social backgrounds among a student group?

Linguistically Oriented Approaches

Examination of emerging approaches to reading will reveal significant differences in linguistic positions, and strangely enough, methods employed often appear to be diametrically opposed.

Most linguistic reading methods can be characterized under one of two general positions, (1) the phonological or sound system approach or (2) the meaning structure approach. From the phonological position, the linguist defines reading as the process of decoding written forms back into the sounds of spoken language. Decoding of *sounds,* not *meanings,* is regarded as the key objective. In fact, some linguists insist that the "meaning-getting" process and the skill-building decoding process should be separated to insure concentration on the decoding skills.

Reading approaches based on linguistic pedagogical principles are not so easily described. Few, if any, could be called "pure" linguistic approaches. The trend in recent years is to incorporate both sound patterning and grammatical structure patterning in the instructional program.

In general, the programs labeled as phono-linguistic approaches reflect the following characteristics:

1. Beginning reading materials are limited to words having regular phonemic sound patterns, i.e., *pat, mat, pin, man, lap;* such irregular forms as *said, have, was, mother,* are withheld until the child has mastered basic spelling patterns.

2. Vocabulary is couched in repetitive sentence patterns. (Nat has a fat cat. A cat sat on the mat. Nat pats the cat.)
3. Content of beginning programs is framed in repetitious sound patterns; most programs concentrate on words which make up a complete sentence but follow the consonant-vowel-consonant patterns (cvc) as in *pat, pin, map.*
4. Focus is on the controlled structuring of linguistic patterns as the child attempts to transfer oral speech to printed forms.

The Meaning-Structure Approach

The structuralist is concerned with spoken language and views reading as a process of interpreting "chunks of meaning" through basic syntactical structures that fit present-day English. Stress is placed on kernal sentences, word order, and signals that mark the function of words. From this point of view, the child should be introduced to reading through whole sentences closely related to the vernacular of child talk. Vocabulary is not strictly controlled and informal patterns, including contractions, are employed.

The position of the structural linguist is reflected in a statement of purpose found in the teacher's edition of the Harper and Row Basic Reading Program for Level Two:

> The immediate purpose of the linguistic exercises is to bring to the child's level of consciousness certain features and patterns in the English language which, unconsciously, the child knows and which he takes into account whenever he speaks. . . . He may be called upon to enlarge the basic parts of a sentence, to experiment with the mobility of adjectives and adverbs, or to compare shifts in meaning with the changing intonational patterns within a given utterance.[2]

Sentence Sound Approach

Another linguistically based approach is reflected in an excerpt from the teacher's edition of Holt, Rinehart and Winston, *Sounds of a Distant Drum:*

> The Sounds of Language reading program uses the melody of language to help children find a sense of sound in printed symbols.

---

[2]Mabel O'Donnel and Byron H. Van Roekel, *All Through the Year* Basic Second Reader, Strand 1 (Evanston, Ill: Harper & Row, 1966), p. 43.

The sound of sense in a sentence is the fundamental sound in our language. It is more important than the sound of any individual word . . . It is easier for children to read whole patterns of words tied together by a strong sentence sound than it is for them to read a list of isolated words.

. . . Immediately after reading "a poem," a child can take the sentences apart, analyze them and put them back together again—because of the miracle of the sentence sound.[3]

ADVANTAGES AND LIMITATIONS

Phonological Approaches

Criticisms of the "pure" phonological approach are usually leveled at the de-emphasis of meaning in the beginning stages of reading. Many authorities feel that reading can become a mechanical pronounciation exercise if word attack skills are approached other than from meaning context, particularly in initial reading stages.

A second criticism is often aimed toward highly structured content and the rigid vocabulary control imposed to maintain consistent and regular spelling patterns. While there may be an element of logic in withholding irregular words such as *said, come, look,* and *once,* which obviously do not have a one-to-one correspondence in letter-sound relationship, the technique violates one of the basic premises of linguistics, that is, (1) reading materials should be couched in the form of meaningful child-like language, and (2) motivation is the key to behavior change.

The question then is simply, "Shall we delay those irregular forms until the child experiences some success, at the risk of watering down material into rather inane content, or shall we present high interest content utilizing whatever irregular forms are needed at the risk of frustrating children with an unrealistic vocabulary load?"

Structural Approaches

Common criticisms of the structure approach focus on vocabulary and the lack of systematic sequential word recognition skills. Critics question whether all children will develop individual techniques needed in "cracking the code" unless they are given specific and systematic instruction.

---

[3]Bill Martin, Jr., *Sounds of a Distant Drum,* Teacher's Edition, Grade 6, The Sounds of Language Series (New York: Holt, Rinehart and Winston, Inc., 1967), pp. TE, 9–10.

Often cited as a weakness in the meaning structure approach is the vocabulary load imposed on bilinguals in beginning reading.

NOT A QUESTION OF EITHER-OR

The logic in both approaches is sound. How can it be otherwise? Vocabulary power depends upon the ability to decode symbols to sound, while building up an ever-increasing stockpile of sight words. But reading words and interpreting ideas are not the same thing. Both the decoding approach and the meaning approach, when interlocked, are aimed toward common objectives.

An eclectic approach to reading embraces the idea that the best of each approach should be combined and adapted to the student's needs.

In the final sense, the success of any approach can be measured only to the degree that the student is empowered to read, motivated to want to read, and inspired to continue to read on his own.

EXTENDED READINGS

Bailey, Mildred Hart. "The Utility of Phonic Generalizations in Grades One Through Six." *The Reading Teacher* 16 (1963):252–258.

Bormuth, John. "Cloze as a Measure of Readability." in *Readings as an Intellectual Activity*, ed. J. Figurel. IRA Conference Proceedings, 8 (1963): 131–134.

Collier, Marilyn. "An Evaluation of Multi-Ethnic Basal Readers." *Elementary English* XLIV (Feb. 1967):152–157.

Durkin, Delores. *Teaching Young Children to Read*. Boston: Allyn & Bacon, Inc., 1972, pp. 308–399.

Emans, Robert. "The Usefulness of Phonic Generalizations Above the Primary Grades." *The Reading Teacher* (Feb. 1967):419–425.

Gray, William S. *On Their Own in Reading*, Rev. ed. Chicago: Scott Foresman & Co., 1960.

Glock, Marvin D. "Developing Clear Recognition of Pupil Purposes for Reading," *The Reading Teacher* 11 (Feb. 1958):165–170.

Goodman, Kenneth S. "A Linguistic Study of Cues and Miscues in Reading." *Elementary English* XXXXII (Oct. 1965): 639–643.

Hall, Robert A. *Sound & Spelling in English*. Philadelphia: Chilton Co., Book Division, 1961.

Heilman, Arthur W. *Phonics in Proper Perspective.* Columbus, Ohio: Charles E. Merrill Publ. Co., 1964, p. 94.

———— and Elizabeth Ann Holmes. *Smuggling Language into the Teaching of Reading.* Columbus, Ohio: Charles E. Merrill Publ. Co., 1972, p. 109.

Hildreth, Gertrude. "The Role of Pronouncing and Sounding in Learning to Read." *Elementary School Journal* LV (Nov. 1954):141–47.

Jones, Daisy Marvel. *Teaching Children to Read.* New York: Harper & Row, 1971, pp. 81–91.

Oaks, Ruth. "A Study of the Vowel Situation in a Primary Vocabulary." *Education* LXXI (May 1952):604–617.

Poole, Irene. "Genetic Development of Articulation of Consonant Sounds in Speech." *Elementary English* XI (June 1934):159–161.

Sabaroff, Rose. "Breaking the Code: What Method?" *Elementary School Journal* 67 (Nov. 1966):95–103.

Schall, Leo M. "Teaching Structural Analysis." *The Reading Teacher* 21 (Nov. 1967):133–137.

Taba, Hilda. "The Teaching of Thinking." *Elementary English* LII (May 1965):534–542.

Wylie, Richard E., and Donald D. Durrell. "Teaching Words Through Phonograms." *Elementary English* XLVII (Oct. 1970):787–791.

CHAPTER 8

Broadening
Reading Experiences

The primary reading program spirals into another level as students move toward intermediate grades. It's a time ripe with opportunity for broadening reading experiences. By this time most children will have acquired skills that empower them to begin reading on their own.

Normally, at this age boys and girls are curious, adventure-seeking beings with boundless energy. If we can harness that energy and provide a qualitative learning environment there is reason to believe they will become self-learners.

Such an environment offers many opportunities for:

1. Inquiry, discovery and choice making in problem-solving activities
2. Involvement in the democratic process through responsible interaction with teachers and peers
3. Encounters that involve the learner in self-seeking, self-pacing, self-assessing experiences
4. Effective interpersonal teacher-to-student and student-to-student communication
5. Responsible, creative expression of ideas both in and out of the classroom.
6. Responsible, critical interpretation of ideas expressed in written and in spoken form
7. Functional usage of both oral and written skills in problem-solving situations
8. Exposure to experiences that develop aesthetic and literary sensitivity which in turn should extend the student's ability to express ideas with color, clarity, and imagination

9. Development of the mechanical skills that enable a student to write, spell, and manage the structure of language so that others can easily interpret his ideas

PROBLEM-CENTERED READING

In contrast to the narrative style used in beginning readers and story books, a more formalized style of presentation is used in science, social studies texts and reference materials. The reading style suitable for *Jack and the Beanstalk* or *Gulliver's Travels* is not appropriate for science content where fact, not fantasy, is involved. Yet, the search for scientific information about the life cycle of a frog in a second grade science book is just as important as reading for scientific data concerning jet propulsion in a junior high school text book.

Speed appropriate for reading dialogue sprinkled with quotation marks won't work for math problems where quantitative and qualitative terms necessitate careful, deliberate reading. Style, speed, and purpose shift when the student is asked to read from two or three sources, not one, to find answers for problems in social studies. The chance is remote that a child will automatically adjust his reading ability to such new purpose without guidance from the teacher.

Guidance in problem-centered reading must be aimed toward assisting the student in the following specialized reading skills:

1. to get accurate and specific details,
2. to grasp the key ideas from the selection,
3. to get a mental "fix" of relationships of time and space,
4. to organize ideas in sequence, and
5. to process what is gleaned from the printed page in light of what is previously known.

Specialized Vocabulary

In the areas of content, vocabulary loads increase. Words appear in new context. The word *times* used in "We have good times at the park," has little in common with the contextual meaning of the same word in "two *times* two," much less 2×2. Synonyms and antonyms become very important to meaning. Ideas expressed in picturesque language such as "Neccessity is the mother of invention," or "Swift as an arrow" defy literal interpretation for many students. These and many other vocabulary skills apply to the specialized words found in the disciplines of each content area.

LEVELS OF THINKING ABILITY

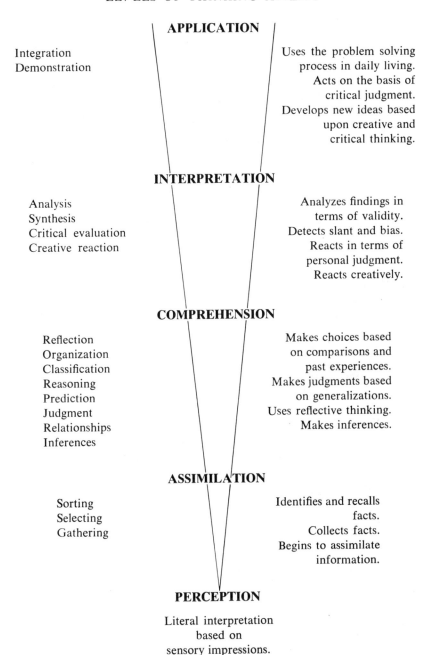

APPLICATION

Integration
Demonstration

Uses the problem solving
process in daily living.
Acts on the basis of
critical judgment.
Develops new ideas based
upon creative and
critical thinking.

INTERPRETATION

Analysis
Synthesis
Critical evaluation
Creative reaction

Analyzes findings in
terms of validity.
Detects slant and bias.
Reacts in terms of
personal judgment.
Reacts creatively.

COMPREHENSION

Reflection
Organization
Classification
Reasoning
Prediction
Judgment
Relationships
Inferences

Makes choices based
on comparisons and
past experiences.
Makes judgments based
on generalizations.
Uses reflective thinking.
Makes inferences.

ASSIMILATION

Sorting
Selecting
Gathering

Identifies and recalls
facts.
Collects facts.
Begins to assimilate
information.

PERCEPTION

Literal interpretation
based on
sensory impressions.

Thinking Levels

Reading for deep understanding is hard work. There are no short cuts. Deep thought demands concentration. We can play games to motivate the student but nothing really happens until the light flashes and he says, "I've got it." When the student begins to play self-challenging games with himself he is on his way as a learner. Motivation acquired through superficial means lasts only as long as the rewards last.

Critical reading demands high-powered concentration that results in the student's ability to read between and beyond the lines, to sort the chaff from the wheat, and to do something with what is read. The skills *can be taught* and the process *must begin early* in primary grades if they are to become habitual.

We could define critical reading in the same way we might define critical thinking. Reading is a thinking process. With considerable risk, we can attempt to describe different levels of thinking as shown on the chart on page 149. Actually we know very little about the thinking process. We can only observe what the individual does or says and make educated guesses about the mental processes involved in his behavior. Nevertheless, there appears to be a hierarchy in levels of thinking that has implications for reading instruction.

Teacher's Questions

It is often said that the master teacher is one who possesses the unique skill of stimulating children's thought through the inquiry process. Perhaps it is the teacher's questioning strategy that determines to a great degree the level of performance in a classroom. Certainly, the level of a child's thinking is critically affected by the quality of the questions that are posed to him and to the verbal interaction he experiences with his teacher and his classmates.

If questions are focused on the *"who," "what," "when," "where,"* convergent thinking is involved. Reading for facts and information is a necessary skill. If, however, questioning techniques never get past that point, or if discussion is limited to a situation where teacher asks and pupil responds, students are apt to remain on the factual level. They may read, but they may not know what to do with what they read.

When questions are aimed toward higher levels of thinking, *"how," "why," "in what way,"* and *"what do you think"* serve as invitations to critical and creative thinking. Divergent thinking probably is initiated as early as kindergarten level when the teacher poses such a question as, "What would you have done if the little Ginger-bread Boy had run away from you?"

USING CONTENT MATERIALS

Assuming you have been convinced that reading in content areas is a specialized reading skill, consider the possibilities and the limitations in the following approaches. Keep in mind the student who is bi-cultural or bi-lingual.

Single textbook approach for entire class

Reading:
Teacher-led discussion. Students take turns reading aloud.

Objectives: Determined by text series.
Activities: Text reading, activities suggested by text, work-sheets.
Evaluation: Test on content of texts.

Modified textbook approach

Reading:
Silent reading. Teacher-led discussion. Some oral reading of text. Some reports read by students. Supplementary reading encouraged.

Common textbook for all students with occasional use of other materials.
Objectives: Determined by teacher.
Activities: Chapters followed through the book with occasional films, and some use of library materials. Occasional group work on activities related to text material. Library table with books provided for spare time reading.
Evaluation: Teacher-made tests, work-sheets, tests on text content.

Problem-centered approach

Reading:
Individualized reading related to unit. Reading-thinking skills stressed through teacher-directed reading of selected materials. Different levels of reading materials used. Multiple texts. Supplementary materials.

Focus: Child-Centered Unit
Objectives: Teacher and students set goals related to an area of study. Questions are posed by students and teacher. Students read to find answers and get information.
Materials: Textbooks, library books, pictures, films, filmstrips, tapes.
Activities: Committee work, individual reference reading, student reports, role-playing, field trips, use of outside resources. Classroom library center with time planned for individual reading.
Evaluation: Carried out on a continuous basis as students read, write, report, and interact with the group.

Problem-centered teaching is based on the scientific method. It implements four steps that guide the student toward a solution to a problem. It sets the stage so that he can:

1. Recognize the problem
2. Collect the facts that relate to the problem
3. Set up possible solutions, test various solutions, and
4. Arrive at conclusions based on fact.

Those four steps could describe a six-week unit of work, yet could serve as the basic steps in a single directed reading lesson. The key words are *involvement, discovery, interaction* and *purpose.* This process is equally appropriate to the teaching of an arithmetic problem, the teaching of a reading lesson, the solving of a science experiment, or the basic plan for a social studies unit.

IMPLEMENTING THE PROBLEM-SOLVING APPROACH

One group of primary teachers planned the year's social studies program around six units of work. Each unit was introduced through a series of questions that revolved around a general theme, *Getting to Know Our Community.*

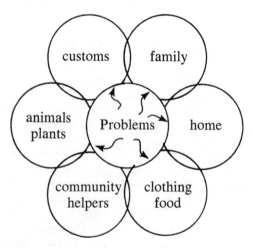

The questions were:
Are all families alike?

What's my job in the family?
Who lives in our community?
Where do we get our food and clothing?
Who are the helpers in our community?
How do animals help us?
Why do people celebrate different things?

Children read books, gathered pictures, saw films, took a field trip through the neighborhood, made booklets, wrote stories, composed charts, painted pictures, and finally made a talking mural that depicted the entire neighborhood including the school. Tape recordings of children telling what they learned about the neighborhood make the mural a "live" picture.

Language concepts were extended, vocabularies has increased, and children had read "to find out." That is the beginning of problem-centered reading.

A fourth grade class became involved in another type of problem-solving unit. The area study was conservation. The unit was titled *Solutions to Pollution*. The problem was called *Abandoned on a Polluted Island*. The objective was to work out a solution to their problem. Solutions took place through the four steps of the scientific approach. They *recognized the problem*. They *collected facts* by reading news items, visiting a recycling plant, talking to conservationists, and reading books. They *set up solutions* by inventing anti-pollution schemes, making a model of the island, drawing up a "solution to pollution" code. They *drew conclusions* as they *discussed, reported,* and *shared ideas.*

ASSESSING INDIVIDUAL NEEDS

As students move beyond primary grades the need for individualized reading experiences increases. It is not unusual to find a grade level range of four or five years among students in a given grade level. We've discussed at length the degrees of differences resulting from background experience, mental-social age, physical factors, as well as educational experiences. Those differences are reflected not only in reading performance but in reading interests as well.

Determining Reading Levels

It is difficult to say which is more damaging—to keep a child reading at frustration level or to place him in material that fails to offer challenge or stimulation. Either is a violation of good reading practice. One of the most important roles for the teacher is to determine at what level the student can read independently, at what level he encounters frustration and at what level he can profit most from reading instruction.

Assessing Individual Reading Performance

A responsibility of crucial significance to the elementary teacher is the assessment of each student's reading level. Too frequently a student becomes "locked in" by being placed in a reading group where materials are unsuited to his capabilities. If teachers are to provide reading instruction geared to specific needs they must determine (1) at what level the student reads independently, (2) at what level he becomes frustrated and unable to proceed on his own, and (3) at what level he can profit most from instruction.

Standardized reading achievement test scores are commonly used as indicators of progress and as a means of placing children in groups. Such scores do give the teacher information about a group of students in relation to age-grade norms. Unfortunately, such scores rarely indicate the nature of a child's reading problem nor do they accurately assess individual levels. The teacher needs specific information regarding the student's ability to attack unknown words, his ability to comprehend what he reads, and the level at which he performs in each of these separate skill areas. This type of assessment can only be done in individual conferences with the student. It is indeed a time consuming process. Fortunately, informal reading inventories are available to aid teachers in carrying out this task in a more objective and less time-consuming process than on a trial and error basis.

Using an Informal Reading Inventory

While reading achievement tests measure global reading levels, an informal reading inventory is a diagnostic technique designed to indicate three levels of reading performance:

1. *Frustration level*—the level at which the student is apt to exhibit tension, uneasiness, finger pointing, word-by-word reading and other manifestations of discomfort. He is unable to answer factual or inferential questions on what he has read or to explain key ideas in his own words.

2. *Instructional level*—in general, although authorities are not in total agreement on this point, the instructional level is defined as that level at which the child can read with at least 95 per cent accuracy in word recognition, and with at least 75 per cent comprehension. It is the

level at which reading textbooks as well as content materials must be aimed.

3. *Independent level*—the level at which the child makes no more than two or three errors in one hundred running words and experiences no difficulty in comprehension. It is at this level that the student can proceed on his own with little or no help.

Different types of informal inventories have been devised. Some are offered in the teacher's editions of basal text series. Others such as the Spache[1] Diagnostic Reading Scales, and the Silveroli[2] Individual Reading Inventory are offered in booklet form. All consist of word lists and selected paragraphs ranging in difficulty from pre-primer level to sixth grade level and beyond. Usually a check list is provided with provisions for recording observations and errors.

With practice, the teacher can administer an individual inventory in ten to twelve minutes. While it may not be necessary to administer the inventory to all students in a class, it is very important that any student demonstrating difficulty in reading should have this type of diagnostic screening. By setting aside periods during the day when class members are busy at seat work, a teacher can schedule individual conferences for testing and for follow-up.

Administering the Informal Inventory

Although inventories vary, the procedure usually is as follows: the student is asked to pronounce words in a graded list. When he misses at least five out of a list of twenty (75%) the teacher discontinues. This level generally would be described as *instructional level*. In Silveroli's[3] Classroom Inventory, after the child reaches the cut-off point (75%), his oral reading level testing should be *started* at the highest level in which he successfully pronounced all (100%) twenty words on the list.

As the student reads the oral paragraphs, the teacher records common errors such as repetitions, omissions, substitutions, insertions, and words not known. Questions follow, measuring comprehension of the material. Here again, 75 per cent comprehension or better is usually regarded as the student's instructional level.

Used along with teacher judgment based on observation of the child, the informal reading inventory provides a means of pinpointing

---

[1]George D. Spache, *Diagnostic Reading Scales* (Monterey: California Test Bureau, 1963).

[2]Nicolas Silveroli, *Individual Reading Inventory* (Dubuque, Iowa: William C. Brown Company, 1970).

[3]Ibid.

reading difficulties as well as determining the level of instructional materials needed. Once determined, the program must provide for each child's reading needs.

The Need to Differentiate Instruction

We cherish diversity among children yet differentiated needs among students pose problems as persistent, and a predictable, as springtime sniffles. No two children are alike and we can expect to find individual differences in ability, in learning modality, and in social and linguistic background; individual tolerance for sustained attention; and individual initiative as a learner.

Competent teachers have always searched for ways to motivate students to go beyond minimum goals of an assignment and to exercise initiative as self-learners. Always too, there has been the challenge of time; time to keep each student bumping his head on the ceiling of his own potential, time to individualize instruction, time to interact meaningfully with each student.

Sometimes, however, a teacher unwittingly falls into traps of his own making. With all the modern facilities, the range of materials and audio-visual aids, the teacher must ask, "Am I actually utilizing the facilities and the resources available to ease time pressures? Am I providing a qualitative environment in which students function as self-teachers? Do I guard my own expertise by utilizing the mechanics of this automated age to carry out the functions for which they are designed?"

EXPANDING READING THROUGH LEARNING CENTERS

Many exciting things have begun to happen in education which represent alternatives to the lock-step pattern that once placed all students in the same mold with a single set of objectives for the entire class. Those alternatives are manifest in practices of team teaching, team learning, student-to-student tutoring, individualized instruction and countless other strategies having to do with "people environment," program organization, and use of materials.

One alternative with promise is the Learning Center concept; not a new notion by any means but a new application of an older concept.

What is a Learning Center?

This is not the science table, the art area, or the reading corner, although these have legitimate purposes. This is not a place where children simply go when an assignment is finished. It's not a reward for good behavior or getting work completed on time. While such corners do serve as interest centers, or enrichment areas, or sanctuaries where children may "meditate" without penalty, the Learning Center we are speaking of serves a much more functional purpose. We're speaking of the Learning Center as being an integral part of the curriculum.

Even if we were to spend the next half day trying to define a Learning Center, I doubt that we could (or should) agree. Someone might define a center in this way: A Learning Center is a place where a student may proceed independently at his own pace, through a programmed assignment with sets of directives that permit him to accomplish a goal or task set up for him.

This definition would be satisfying to the proponents of the behavioristic position based on the Skinnerian theory of stimulus-response. A more current title, or a broader concept might be called *Receptive Learning*. The rationale behind this approach is that learning is change in habitual behavior. Changes in behavior occur through four incentives—*drive, stimulus, response, reward.* Convergent thinking is involved. The target is predetermined. The behavioral goal is set and can be measured objectively by the student's performance.

Using this definition, a Learning Center can be set up to teach, reinforce and make habitual, selected skills in reading such as:

– letter-sound relationships (coding skills)
– specific comprehension skills; *Find the word that means the same as—, Underline the sentence that tells where—,* etc.
– spelling, handwriting, dictionary skills and an endless list of other related skills can be easily programmed into such a center.

Games, educational devices, teacher-made work sheets, as well as commercial tapes and records make this a feasible activity. With cassette tapes to record teacher directives, the center provides drill and reinforcement.

Of course we could define a Learning Center in another way; as an area designed to encourage students to discover new concepts for themselves through observation, investigation, experimentation, and problem-solving experiences. We would probably call this *Discovery Learning,* the rationale being based on Perception Theory, stressed particularly by Piaget, who believes that learning is basically a perceptual processing. He would have us get children very much involved in concrete first-hand experiences where the student makes many discoveries for himself, by trial and error and by problem solving.

In such a center, targets are not singular. Open-endedness and divergent thinking are stressed. Students are given a wide array of materials, sources of information and reading references in order to discover new concepts. Such a center would be concerned with:

- literary experiences (sensitivity and appreciation)
- interpretation (critical-creative reading)
- production of creative writing
- problem-solving reading tasks—in science, social studies, and other content areas.

The key words here are *involvement, investigation, interaction, communication, problem solving, invention.*

Bruner,[4] the eloquent spokesman for Discovery Learning, says opportunities for discovery are imbedded in the context of what has already been learned. He implies that there isn't such a thing as *pure discovery;* that the process of learning and thinking is a matter of leaving gaps here and there which the student can close meaningfully through self-discovery aided by knowledge about problems that he already possesses. We can build a good case, in either approach, for providing a wide variety of tapes, records, models, and live experiences. Perhaps we can never agree upon a definition of a Learning Center but we probably agree that the center can serve as an area designed to place the student in a situation where he is able to:

1. Function as a self-learner
2. Work at a rate and level consistent with his capability
3. Encounter experiences meaningful to him
4. Tackle a problem where he can anticipate success
5. Use a wide variety of learning resources in the solution of his problem
6. Explore possibilities
7. Make choices
8. Receive reinforcement and feedback
9. Know that he has been successful

Extends Time for One-to-One Relationships

We need to search for ways to:

1. Free the teacher from the closed role of decision-maker.
2. Free the student to set his own pace—allow him to proceed

---

[4]J. S. Bruner, *The Process of Education* (Cambridge, Massachusetts: Harvard University Press, 1960).

SUGGESTED FLOOR PLAN FOR CLASSROOMS
UTILIZING ACTIVITY CENTERS

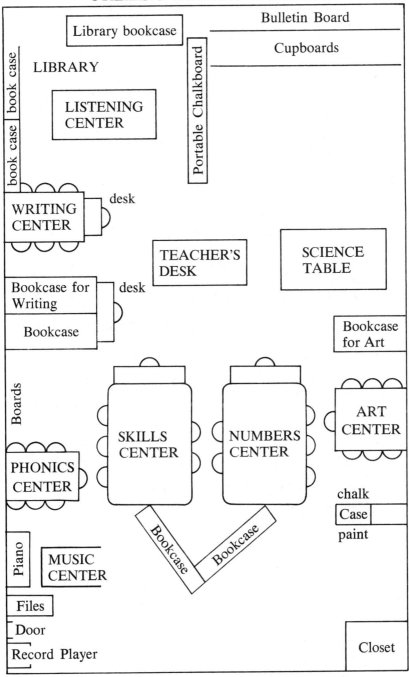

without signals from the teacher, or having to wait for classmates to finish the same task (of course, a machine or a programmed reader can do that).

3. Get the student to take initiative for his own learning—become an aggressive learner, not a passive one. (Programmed readers, no matter how well designed, can't do that!)

4. Get the student into the inquiry habit—to become a questioner, a seeker, a person who wants answers, knows where to look to find information, has the skills and know how to use reference sources, and then, uses them.

Neither machine, nor programmed readers, nor films, nor books can do that—only teachers can. This we'd have to call "teacher power."

The teacher serves such a vital role in these last two areas that it makes sense to see how the organizational patterns in the classroom can put "teacher power" to work in the most advantageous way. We need to utilize every source to do those things that can be done mechanically or that can be programmed in order to extend the teacher's time to interact with students, to guide and counsel them, and to give them individual help, particularly in reading.

The Learning Center is a means of accomplishing many goals, but three in particular:

1. Extending time for one-to-one relationship with students by personalized teaching on tape.

2. Extending time for skill training by utilizing well-designed programmed materials.

3. Enriching and extending concepts through problem-solving experiences set up in a Learning Center.

If we believe that there must be a deliberate balance in the reading program, we need to look to each area to see where a Learning Center can aid in maintaining that balance.

Types of Centers

All centers for self-learning either directly or indirectly involve reading. Those directly concerned would include the following:

1. **A listening center:** Teacher-prepared tapes correlated with teacher-prepared work sheets for practice in reading skills. Commercial tapes and records for story telling, and other literary experience listening activities.

2. **Library center for individual choice reading:** A carpeted area surrounded with shelves of books, categorized and color-coded to aid students in making selections and locating books at his level.
3. **Skills center:** A collection of games and teaching tools available for aid in word building skills, spelling, and other reading and writing.
4. **A film viewing center:** Where students may operate film strip projectors and other audio-visual equipment.
5. **Creative writing center:** Pictures and other materials to help children write independently. Word lists, word charts, dictionaries and other vocabulary needs.
6. **Science center:** Books, materials, specimens, models, magnets, microscope, tapes, film strips, etc.

Listening Time

Children become sensitive to literary quality only by being exposed to good books. What better way than to provide time for children to listen to tapes and records of stories and poems read by voices that give beauty and feeling to literary selections? Second language learners particularly need much time for this type of experience.

Is There a Way to Use Learning Centers in Problem-Centered Reading?

Probably this is the area where centers make the greatest contribution. A center provides a means of dealing with concepts on a self-discovery basis.

The teacher can prepare tapes to guide the student through a sequence of activities as he uses many sources of reference. The diagram on page 162 suggests possible steps through which this can be done. Problem-solving situations relating to science or social living can be implemented.

1. Student begins sequence at listening post; orientation, introduction of problem, lead-in questions and directives for procedure (pretaped by teacher).
2. Guide Card; serves to assist student in understanding the problem-solving task; clues information, and directives for problem assignment.
3. Observation, investigation, experimentation; involves pictures, specimens, models, live animals or plants, games, manipulation devices or any other materials pertinent to the problem.

4. Check point; conference with aide or teacher for interaction, questioning, reactions to observation, and directions for next activity.

5. Reading to find out: student has choice of pictures, multi-level textbooks, weekly readers, library books, and/or teacher prepared reading material related to the concepts involved.

6. Concept Development; Task assignment with optional learning activities to help student make discoveries about the problem; involves paper-pencil tasks, construction, illustration, making booklets, assembling pictures and materials, completing work sheets or any suitable means of assisting the student in demonstrating his understanding of the concept(s) involved in the problem.

7. Teacher-student conference; teacher and student interaction for purpose of communication, evaluation, and reinforcement.

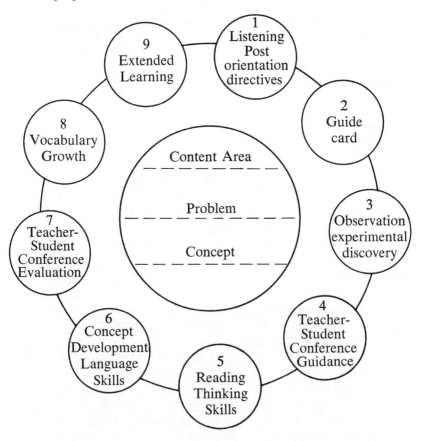

8. Vocabulary and language activity; student works with new words, writes them in individual dictionary.
9. Extended experience; student has options for extended experiences in related areas; independent reading, art work, film strips, pictures and/or individual projects.

What if the Classroom is Small and There is No Room for Centers?

Shoe-box reading may be the answer. Materials such as would be used in phonic skill centers, in the creative writing center and so on can be boxed in see-through plastic shoe boxes and be checked out by students. If the listening center is no more than a single tape recorder with a pair of head-phones, students can utilize cassette tapes especially prepared by the teacher for a one-to-one experience with the teacher even though it must sometimes be by remote control.

Finally, we must ask again, "Where do we go from here to assure that all boys and girls, regardless of ethnic background, socio-economic status, or language difference, can and will claim their *right to read?*" Part of the answer is to assure that the teacher is competent as a reading instructor. But that is only part of the full circle of accountability. Equally important is the provision for one-to-one relationships between teacher and pupil so that assessment, diagnosis, guidance, and instruction go hand in hand.

Effective teaching-learning situations must provide a means, a time, and a place where each child can develop his uniqueness. In the end, reading is a highly personalized act. In this role the teacher becomes more of an "enabler" than a teacher. Gibran said it eloquently:

> No man can reveal to you aught but that already lies half asleep in the dawning of your knowledge. The teacher . . . if he is indeed wise does not bid you enter the house of his wisdom, but rather leads you to the threshold of your own mind.[5]

The teacher, in the role of instructor, guide, counselor, and mediator of the culture seeks to enable all children to reach the threshold of their capabilities.

---

[5]Kahlil Gibran, *The Prophet* (New York: Alfred A. Knopf, 1969), p. 56.

EXTENDED READINGS

Abramson, Paul, ed. "Lake Normandy School." *Grade Teacher* 85 (May-June 1968):91.

Allen, R. B. "Grouping Through Learning Centers." *Childhood Education* 45 (December 1968):200–3.

Cisco, G., and D. Lake. "Learning Laboratory." *School and Community* 56 (February 1970):17.

Christianson, B. J., and L. Holliday. "Learning Centers That Work." *Instructor* 79 (October 1969):135.

"CMSC's Self-Instruction Center." *School and Community* 56 (April 1970): 16–7.

"Developing a Learning Center, in ABE." *Adult Leadership* 19 (June 1970):48–50.

Drummond, Darrel. "The Learning Center: A Chance for Every Child." *National Elementary Principal* 50 (September 1970):31–39.

Gottardi, L. "Instruction Media Center Services in the Nongraded Elementary School." *AV Instructor* 16 (April 1971):30.

"Flexible Approach to an Independent Study Facility." *Educational Technology* 10 (December 1970):29–31.

Grindeland, and R. Bliss. "Developing a Center for Science." *Science Teacher* 36 (October 1969):67–8.

Hillerick, R. L. "Creative Learning Center." *Elementary School* 69 (February 1969):259–64.

Killough, K. "Matzke Resource Center." *AV Instructor* 51 (February 1970):61.

"Learning Labs Spur School Back to Movement." *American Vocation* 46 (January 1971):32–4.

Like, D. W. "More on Learning Resource Centers." *Childhood Education* 46 (January 1970):209–12.

McNeill. "Individualized Learning Center." *Kentucky School Journal* 47 (March 1969):20–1.

Miller, N. "Learning Resources Center; Its Role in Education." *AV Instructor* 16 (May 1971):48.

Nygen, B. M. "Student Self-directed Study Centers." *Minnesota Journal of Education* 49 (September 1968):19–20.

"Planning Your Resource Center." *American School and University* 43 (September 1970):24–8.

Reuter, A. "Listening Experiences: Instructional Materials Center Dial-A-Tape System Advances Learning." *Elementary English* 46 (1969): 905–6.

Slobodian, J., and E. Steward. "Reading Materials Center." *Michigan Education Journal* 13 (May 1966):31.

Taber, Julian. *Learning and Programmed Instruction.* Chicago: Addison-Wesley Publishing Company, 1965, pp. 62–112.

Vallet, R. E. "Learning Resource Center for Exceptional Child." *Exceptional Child* 36 (March 1970):527–30.

Way, A. "Reading Center Fills Needs." *Wisconsin Journal of Education* 99 (April 1967):14.

Index

Ability group instruction, 53, 54, 56
Accountability, 51
Age, chronological, 43
Artley, A. S., 24
Assessment of development and abilities, 63–68
Auditory perception, 61, 62, 70, 73–78

Barrett, Thomas C., 90
Basal reader programs, 139–42
Berstein, B., 11
Bilingual education, 4–5, 22–23
Black dialect, 38–40
Bloom, B. S., 8, 9
Bruner, J. S., 158
Bond, Guy L., 89
Bumpas, Faye L., 126

Cassels, Louis, 1
Child, entering school, 46–50
Classroom experience, 109–10
Cognitive development, 62–63
Communication, 103–05
Content, in textbooks and materials, 119–20, 151–52
Conceptual relationship understandings, 61
Consonant sounds, 36
Critical reading, 150

Dallmann, Martha, 2
DeBoer, John J., 2
Deutsch, Martin, 10, 74
Dialects, 29, 37–40
Dictation, 110–12, 116
Discovery learning, 157, 158
Durrell, Donald D., 90
Dykstra, Robert, 89

Egocentric stage of development, 49–50
Ego-involved process in language experience, 105
English, as second language, 20–21
Evaluation (see Assessment; Tests)
Experiences, personal, 109–10, 120–21

Failure, of students, 9–12
Freeman, A. M., 74
Frostig, Marianne, 69, 84

Gibran, Kahil, 163
Gladney, Mildred R., 107
Goins, Jean Turner, 89
Goodman, Kenneth, 107

Grade level instruction, 53
Grammatical patterns, 19, 20, 36–37, 39

Handicapped children, perceptually, 9
Harper and Row Basic Reading Program for Level Two, 143
Heilman, Arthur W., 53, 86
Hester, Kathleen B., 90
Hildreth, Gertrude, 90
Holt, Rinehart and Winston, *Sounds of a Distant Drummer*, 143–44

Illiteracy, 1–2, 3
Indian education, 11–12, 127–28
Individualized instruction, 53, 54, 56
Informal reading inventory, 154–56
Instruction in reading
    balanced approach, 99
    differentiated, 52–53, 156
Interference problems, in dialect differences, 33–40

Katz, Phyllis, 74
Key vocabulary approach, 113–14
Kirk, Samuel A., 24, 69, 85–86
Kobrick, Jeffrey, 4

Lamb, Pose, 17, 18
Lamoreaux, Lillian A., 105
Language, 17–20, 21–22
Language assessment, tests for, 68
Language experience approach, 104, 105–09, 122–25
Language-handicapped student, limitations, 106–08
Language power, 51
Learning centers, 156–63
Learning experiences, 116–18
Lee, Doris M., 105
Letter knowledge, 89–94
Letter-sound relationships, 31
Library, 127
Linguistic approaches, 16–17, 102, 142–45
    codes, 11
Listening time, 161
Literary reading, for pleasure, 100, 125–28

McCarthy, James J., 69
Macnamera, John, 25
Maslow, A. H., 50
Materials, for instruction, 101, 127–28